THE COLLINGRIDGE BOOK OF

# Dried and Pressed Flowers

JANE DERBYSHIRE & RENEE BURGESS

## Optimum Books

*This edition published by Optimum Books 1981*

*First published in 1975 by*
*The Hamlyn Publishing Group Limited*
*London · New York · Sydney · Toronto*
*Astronaut House, Feltham, Middlesex, England*
© *The Hamlyn Publishing Group Limited 1975*
*ISBN 0 600 33952 1*

*Filmset in Monophoto 10 pt. Bembo by Tradespools Limited,*
*Frome, Somerset, England*
*Printed in Italy*

ACKNOWLEDGEMENTS
*Line drawings by Marilyn Day*
*Dried flower photography by Martin Rice*
*Pressed flower photography by John Seymour*

PRINTED IN ITALY          ISBN 0 600 33952 1

# Contents

LONDON:
MILNER AND SOWERBY,
44, PATERNOSTER ROW,
1867.

# Drying and Preserving Flowers

I dedicate my part of this
book to my friends

JANE DERBYSHIRE

*. . . Methought that of these visionary flowers*
*I made a nosegay, bound in such a way*
*That the same hues, which in their natural bowers*
*Were mingled or opposed, the like array*
*Kept these imprisoned children of the Hours*
*Within my hand, – and then, elate and gay,*
*I hastened to the spot whence I had come,*
*That I might there present it! – Oh! to whom?*

SHELLEY, 'THE QUESTION'

# What's It All About?

First times are something special. Times to remember. And, though it is now many years ago, I still clearly recall the excitement of the very first time I successfully preserved a whole fragile spray of pink-and-white-petalled roses; single ones, so that when they were placed in a shallow porcelain shell you truly couldn't tell that I had not picked them moments before from the garden.

As you read through the following pages I hope I shall be able to lead you to a number of first times of your own, and that as you go on to preserve perfectly the colour and the contour in every petal of, say, a bunch of mixed zinnias bought from a street barrow in August or the first delicious spring posy from the garden, this most rewarding and ever remarkable aspect of flowers and their arrangement will bring you the greatest joy.

The gentle, very sentimental age of Queen Victoria is specially associated with flower preservation. Young ladies in our grandmothers' day dried flowers, grasses, and seedheads for their winter rooms. They skeletonised leaves by a painstaking method which included quicklime, and lovingly pressed pansies in books. But flowers had been preserved for sentiment and decoration long before this. I was interested to read that azure-blue delphiniums brought out a year or so ago from the still darkness of an Egyptian tomb were as clear a blue as on the day they were placed there as a loving tribute to a pharaoh. Every woman, of every race and age, has something of the squirrel in her character—an urge to preserve for tomorrow just a little of what she is enjoying today. Should you need any proof of this, just notice how home freezers have caught on during the past few years!

Today's methods of flower preservation are as up-to-the-minute as the modern deep-freeze, and not merely such easy flowers as delphiniums can be successfully preserved. You can keep forget-me-nots, mimosa, chrysanthemums, roses, azaleas—the list is almost endless. By the way, in this half of the book I will be referring to 'flower' preservation but this also includes foliage, fruit, and any of the other natural forms used so imaginatively nowadays by the flower arranger. See beauty in all things—the winter-bleached branchlets of tall weeds can be as lovely as a hothouse blossom in the rightness of their setting.

## A Wider Repertoire

Although I would be the last person in the world to suggest that preserved plant materials can ever take over from the lively beauty of fresh materials, they do have their moments. A few preserved items certainly widen the flower arranger's repertoire, and

make invaluable and perfect accompaniments to central heating, with its difficulties for fresh flowers. They are delightful for miniature arrangements, and preserved flowers, requiring no water, will never spoil the surface of a piece of fine furniture.

People living in flats, or houses with only very small gardens, require their expensively-bought or frugally-picked fresh flowers to last for as long as possible. Preserved, they will go on to delight for many weeks, often months, possibly years—even difficult subjects such as hellebores. You can keep a special treasure such as a flower from a wedding bouquet, or perhaps the whole bouquet itself. With a few boxes of carefully preserved items you can produce inexpensive and original presents, or good money-spinners for flower club sales tables, church bazaars, and so on. Once you start you will wonder, like the new freezer owner, how you ever existed before.

On the whole, fresh flowers do not last at all well in central heating, do they? Preserved flowers and leaves do. They revel in it. They can be arranged in a thousand and one ways, including some which would not be possible with fresh material. Another interesting aspect can be the making of pictures, collages, calendars, etc., and many arrangers specialise in these. And a preserved flower arrangement in a wall vase never, never dribbles!

## The Choice of Containers

The choice of container is important. And what holds the stems in place? Do designs of preserved things differ very much from designs of fresh material? These are some of the questions the beginner to preserving must ask herself.

Containers should be chosen in exactly the same manner, and for exactly the same reasons, as when arranging fresh flowers, bearing in mind colours, proportion of plant material to container, bases, and so on. There are, however, one or two things to which I would like to draw particular attention in this respect.

Though the preserved plant material will look largely as it did in life, it will in fact be exceptionally light in weight if it has been preserved by any method which extracts the moisture. With this feather-light material one can sometimes take advantage of very fragile and delicate containers, even glass ones or heirloom china. Without the necessity for water, the container itself is lighter than it would be with fresh flowers, and if very top-heavy items are to be included in the design it may be necessary to weight the container to prevent the whole arrangement tipping over.

Tall, lightweight containers can be filled with dry sand or pebbles topped with melted candle wax; the stemholder (foam, chicken wire, or pinholder) is placed on top of the wax before it sets. If you wish your design to be fairly permanent you can pour candle wax over the lower part of the stems when the arrange-

*Gay yellow aconites, each set in a dog-Toby ruff of green, are arranged early in the year with skeletonised holly leaves and small begonia foliage. Both aconites and begonia were preserved in desiccant. Notice how clear glass suggests water and deceives the eye into thinking that these are fresh flowers.*

ment is complete. A piece of lead hooked over the back of a lightweight container can be helpful, or even your flower scissors can be positioned at the back to act as a counterweight in an emergency! If the design is a good one, however, it should be stable within itself, with as much weight of material at the back as at the front.

Now that it is possible to achieve such vibrant, life-like colours in preserved flowers (and also usually permissible to dye and artificially colour plant material, even for show work in Britain) containers do not always have to be very gentle in colour. For modern work in particular, eye-catching effects can be won by using stark, bold shapes and madly coloured flowers and containers. On the whole, though, preserved plant life seems to look most comfortable and at home in quiet settings. Remember that in competition work plant material must at all times predominate, which means that the container, accessories, etc. *must* play second fiddle to the flowers.

## Give It a Base

Bases of various sorts have long been used in association with fresh flower-pieces. Similarly they can and should be used in conjunction with preserved material. They must be of colour and texture to complement the plant forms and not be so small as to be of no account or, a more common fault, too large so that they are over-eye-catching. Old or new wooden floorboards are of good visual interest and can be sawn to fit most bold designs, and stained with shoe dye or polish. Other ideas include plain-coloured table mats, broken pieces of marble, metal trays, hardboard cut to a shape and either covered with fabric or painted, or a shape made from a sheet of emery paper or sandpaper.

## What Holds the Stems?

When we are making a fresh flower arrangement we have to provide some support for the stems inside the container. The support, often called the mechanics of the arrangement, may be a pinholder, a well-pinholder, soft 2-in. gauge chicken wire crumpled up, or one of the range of moisture-holding materials available. All these can be used equally well for supporting the stems of preserved materials, though, except for the smallest designs, chicken wire will nearly always be found necessary in conjunction with the other items.

The chicken wire will have to be a trifle more closely crumpled than when making a fresh flower arrangement, so as to hold securely the very thin stalks of things which have been preserved in a desiccant, and it will need to be held firm in the container with a rubber band. I should warn you of the general unsuitability of very small-mesh chicken wires, which are too difficult to crumple. If the pins of a pinholder will not hold the slim, brittle, rock-hard stalks of dried items, a little dome, made of closely crumpled chicken wire will be found useful. Similarly one can use chicken wire, or a piece of tinfoil or thin plastic, over a foam block for extra security. The fine mesh bags in which oranges and sprouts are sold at supermarkets are also excellent, especially if sprayed an earthy colour.

There are a number of plastic foams on the market specially designed for arrangements of preserved plant materials. They are sold in blocks which can be

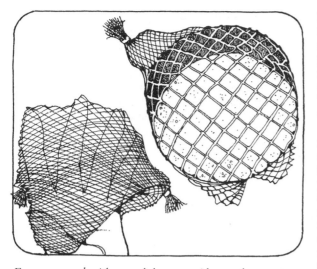

*Foam, covered with a mesh bag, provides good support.*

cut to the shape of any container with a sharp knife, and also come in rounds, hearts, rings, etc. They do not absorb moisture. If you experience difficulty in positioning stems make holes in the foam with a thick wire or stem. It is really worth trying each product for yourself to see which you prefer, or indeed whether you would rather work with one of the softer water-retaining foams, which can be used dry as well as moist. One such foam can be obtained complete with useful round, interlocking plastic box containers, as well as in special plastic holders for screwing or sticking to walls, driftwood, or bases.

Heavy pinholders, purpose made with fewer but longer pins, are invaluable for supporting blocks of any foam; if one uses ordinary pinholders for this purpose they often get blocked up. Foams will hold well on a pool of melted wax. Always bring the foam block above the level of the container's rim for greater ease of stem placing. Hold the flowers low down on the stems and press them firmly into the foam. Last, central placements can sometimes be difficult to position and it is often helpful to stick them in place with a blob of gum or adhesive.

As with all flower arrangements, it is vital that the mechanics are absolutely secure before stems are inserted. If a pinholder needs to be stuck down to a container I often use a flower clay designed for this job. This adheres to dry clean surfaces and will also mould in the hand into suitable shapes for supporting stems. The mechanics can generally be hidden with stones, reindeer moss or other mosses, pieces of cork bark, driftwood, fruit, cones, seeds, leaves, recessed flowers, and so on. For permanent designs you can work straight into a mound of made-up Polyfilla or plaster of Paris before it hardens; a little chicken wire set in the mixture can be most helpful.

## Using False Stems

On the whole, flowers and foliage will be preserved complete with their own stems, but where this is not possible use either the heads for calendars, swags, floral balls, etc., or make false stems with florist's wire (disguised with florist's tape), cocktail sticks, pieces of branch, slim house plant stakes, cane, drinking straws, or hollow stems from other dried material.

Many a lovely arrangement has been spoiled when false stems were either of the wrong colour or length or, just as important, the wrong thickness. Imagine a freesia with a false stem the thickness of that of a delphinium, or the funny bright green colour of a plant stake. Similarly, a very straight-stemmed flower in a naturalistic setting looks uneasy if provided with a false whirlygig stalk. Try to make everything appear as life-like as possible, except in ultra-modern designs for which off-beat, unlikely, bizarre colours and shapes may be acceptable and indeed desirable, and for which stems can spiral or contort as they will to give liveliness to a design.

## Consider the Stems

Placing and anchoring a preserved flower stem can be difficult. Anything with a hard stem is far easier to position in foam and/or wire than on a pinholder. Make matters easier for yourself by considering the stem before you preserve the flower. A little bend at the end of a stem can make it impossible to position, so cut it off before preserving. Where possible, leave stems attached to flowers. Cut them down to a variety of suitable lengths before preserving. Most stalks will preserve even in desiccants, the exceptions are those of an extremely squashy nature, or any which become so thin in drying that they will not support the flower head. In this latter category come helichrysum (everlasting flower).

Before preserving helichrysums, provide false stems by making a little hook at one end of a piece of florist's stub wire and passing the wire gently down through the face of the flower into the top of the stem, so that the hook is caught and hidden by the centre of the flower. False stems for leaves are made by taping a wire or twig up the back of the leaf. A little run of glue under the wire will make it extra strong. Or you can make a stitch through the back of the main rib with stub wire, leaving one end of the wire shorter to bring down and twist round the other, and disguise with florist's tape of a suitable colour. Freezer tape may also be used, and will take spray-on colour if desired.

Pine cones are useful but, having no stem, must often be provided with one to give security. Take two stub wires (the thickness depending on the size of cone) and place these opposite each other, one at the front, one at the back of the lower scales, and twist firmly together at both sides. Bring the wires down

*False stems are easily made with florist's wire.*

and twist together to form a stem. Tape with florist's tape.

Stems of wire etc., for dried fruits such as gourds and pomegranates, are best put in place when the fruit has dried. You may need to get your husband to drill a couple of small holes at the base of the fruit for a thickish stub wire to be passed through and twisted together to form a stem, or drill one hole for a wooden stake. Nuts can be drilled similarly and wired in clusters.

If natural flower stems are to be wired, do this before drying. Always try to handle preserved flowers by their stems, holding them just beneath the head. Stiffer wires will be required for thick-stemmed flowers and finer ones for thin. Remember the higher the gauge number, the finer the wire. Stems such as honeysuckle, larkspur and iris dry easily and can be kept on hand for making false stems for other flowers. To provide unusually swirly stems on which to pin or glue flower heads use curly pieces of natural cane bought at do-it-yourself or craftwork shops. To alter the curves, soak the cane overnight, re-shape, and then allow to dry again. A drinking straw used as a stem can be curved slightly by pushing florist's wire through it. Clear drinking straws can make ethereal stem effects in glass containers. Dried flowers with very thin stems are difficult to position on pinholders and it is beneficial to press them into a short length of thicker stalk cut and preserved from some other flower, preferably one with a hollow stem; or a piece of thick leaf can be doubled over the base of the stem and taped into position.

## Hints on Arranging

When arranging preserved flowers you will find that a more pleasing life-like effect is created if, whenever possible, flowers are positioned in such a way that the majority of their faces and buds, or at least the tilt of a petal here and there, look upwards instead of down. Make the fullest play with every appealing upward curve in a stem or slight ripple in a springing leaf. Very straight stems tend to give a static effect. Downward-facing flowers can look sad and lifeless.

Arrange preserved flowers as naturally as possible, in containers and in designs similar to those you would use if arranging the same things picked fresh. There would be no place in the liking of most people for an arrangement of primroses with chrysanthemums or spring blossoms with autumn berries, though preserved and fresh flowers and leaves in harmony do have a liveliness and character which is tremendously pleasing. Oddly enough, in flower pictures, swags, Victorian-type domes, and in very mixed flower designs, the flowers of all seasons seem to marry well. One cannot really generalise, and we must decide for ourselves what seems to 'go' and what seems to lack accord.

When preserving, do make sure that you include some material which is fine and pointed and useful for making outlines, some bold well-shaped flowers and leaves which are rather rounder in appearance for central eye-catching positions, and bits and pieces midway in form and colour to link the two extremes. Many preserved designs appear dull because they are made up of too much that is spiky and thin; one can see right through them and there is nothing to give impact or to catch the lively curiosity of the eye. It is particularly important in preserved designs to have a good number of clean-cut 'impact' flowers placed confidently through the arrangement so that the eye is led easily about it.

## Pedestals and Large Arrangements

When planning a pedestal or other very large arrangement of preserved plant forms, aim to make your mechanics extra firm. I always use one or two blocks of foam held on long-pinned pinholders with a covering of chicken wire. Hook the latter round the rim of the container or round projecting bits on the pedestal, and put two large, broad rubber bands over the lot, or similarly secure with string or florist's reel wire.

It is surprising how springy a large mass of preserved items can be. I think you will find it useful to crunch the chicken wire more closely in those places where extra-thin stems are likely to be positioned, perhaps easing wider spaces in the wire towards the front for thicker stalks. If a few fresh flowers or leaves are to be added, use water-filled florist's tubes in suitable positions, or make use of small water con-

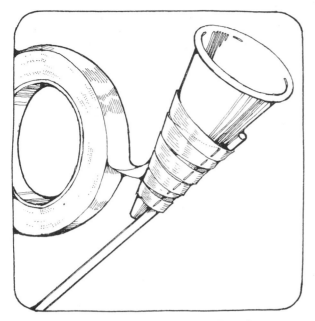

tainers taped to canes, stems, or bamboo sticks with florist's binding tape or transparent adhesive tape. Suitable containers are such things as orchid tubes, cigar tubes, or tablet holders. Spray-paint these containers and the tape in some unobtrusive drab colour to merge with the preserved things.

Similar tubes, filled with dry plastic foam, can be used when adding dried subjects to an arrangement which is basically of fresh material. Florist's tubes of all sizes are easily filled with any soft foam if the tube is pressed firmly, straight down on to the block of foam. Otherwise tubes can be filled with chicken wire or even sprigs of conifer to assist the positioning of the stems.

*A kneeler made for competition in a class asking for a mock-embroidered church kneeler. Roses, anemones, toadstools, hydrangea, acorns, fuchsia and bead-like soft-purple berries of callicarpa show the wide range of flowers and other plant material it is possible to preserve. A slice of polystyrene, covered with embroidery canvas and edged neatly with gold metal ribbon, makes a suitable base on which to 'embroider'. Such designs can be attractive when churches are decorated for flower festivals.*

*Tubes taped to sticks make containers for fresh flowers.*

## Collages and Pictures

When making pictures, calendars, collages, swags, etc., it is often necessary only to preserve flower heads, sections of seedhead, individual leaves; these are stuck directly on to the base of wood, card, silk, linen, hardboard, polystyrene tile, or what you will. I use a light adhesive such as Uhu or Copydex for the purpose.

For larger pictures etc., and things in which greater depth is required, use a dry foam, covered with chicken wire or stuck to the backing, as a support for the plant material. When designing plaques and swags, bases made of pegboard, thin plywood, or hardboard can be cut to the required shape and painted with matt emulsion paint, or covered with seeds, bark, velvet, coarse linen, or any fabric you fancy. The plant material is then wired or glued on, the holes in pegboard being particularly handy for the former method.

Both thin and thick cords, or nylon stockings, can provide a base for a fine garland, but a thicker one is better achieved by wiring plant material to a roll of chicken wire filled with moss and bound firm with fine wire. A circular wire frame bought from your florist or flower club, or an old embroidery frame or lampshade ring, or even one of those wire hangers on which clothes come back from the dry cleaners, may be wired with evergreens, such as holly and golden yew, nuts, cones, and preserved flowers and fruits for Christmas.

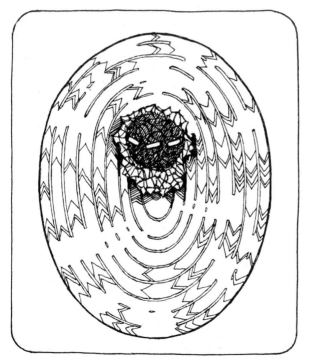

*Foam and wire support the material on a wall hanging.*

A straight swag in Grinling Gibbons' style can be made by wiring plant material to a folded magazine, which is used as a base. Hanging arrangements for walls can be made by wiring a block of plastic foam covered with chicken wire, or painted cooking foil, to a base made from a woven mat, a handleless basket, a piece of heavily ridged cork bark, or a section of mossy tree bark. Into the design you could perhaps work preserved pussy willow, sprays of mimosa, violets and small yellow narcissi in the spring, with a couple of wadding birds; in autumn small gold chrysanthemums with colouring foliage, corn ears, a few seedheads, and perhaps an empty nest. Such designs will last for months and bring much pleasure.

## Like a Ship in a Bottle

Beautifully preserved Victorian-looking decorations of roses, delphiniums, pansies, ferns, etc., can be bought in British shops, delightfully displayed under domes or in glass jars. These are the easiest things in the world to make for yourself at little cost apart from the cost of the jar. Nice clear glass or plastic storage jars can be bought at kitchen shops, and sweet jars from sweet shops. I suppose you could even use a small fish tank. Victorian cases which once held stuffed birds, or modern reproductions of them, or a round fish-bowl or fruit bowl, might be pressed into service with a lid made from transparent kitchen film to keep the dust out. Disguise the overlap with a broad silk cord or a band of velvet ribbon matching the flowers. It is easiest if the opening at the top of the jar is large enough to get your hand into, see illustration on page 21.

If you are right-handed, arrange the flowers and leaves in your left hand, using a tiny container, a pile of Polyfilla afterwards sprayed some soft colour, or a little block of foam on a pinholder, to hold them in place. If the flowers are stemless, press them into a small cone of foam and anchor them in with dabs of glue or, better still, wire them as described for helichrysums, page 7. Finally, gently lower the flower-piece into the jar, sticking it into place with a good blob of wax or glue.

A variation is to cover a lump of flower arranging clay or foam with a couple of curved pieces of cork bark or mossy tree bark, making a container for the flowers (you can buy cork bark from many flower club sales tables and some florists). It is best to arrange the items in a warm, dry atmosphere, as soon as possible after preserving.

Pictures under glass are made in a similar way, sticking the design straight on to the fabric or card backing and perhaps decorating with ribbon bows, then covering with the glass as quickly as possible. Such designs will last for many years if kept out of strong light and away from damp.

## New Flowers from Old

The larger flower shops offer a wide range of contrived flowers made up from various plant forms. It is amusing and perfectly feasible to make your own. Pine cones, for instance, can be useful beginnings because you can stick such things as individual eucalyptus leaves, pine needles, preserved flower petals, honesty seed pods or 'moons', dried skins of avocado pears, or even coloured grasses or grass stems, down between the scales.

Wire preserved magnolia leaves, laurel, or lily-of-the-valley leaves around a poppy seedhead or teasel to make a daisy-like flower; spray it a new colour if you like. Wire and tape pieces of sweet corn sheath in a petal-like manner on a stem round a few grass heads, or use loops of aspidistra like petals, or make them into a romantic bow to decorate a garland. Wire up individual Chinese lanterns to make new flower shapes.

Ideas are endless once you begin to contrive. New textures can be achieved—if you like this sort of thing—by lightly brushing over a preserved leaf with glue and then sprinkling sand or fine seeds over it. Large exotic-looking flowers can be made by sticking heads of grasses, wheat, sweet corn sheaths, or overlapping verbascum leaves in a flower shape, using half a small dry foam ball as the flower centre and covering this with stuck on lentils or split dried peas. Stems of cane are easily inserted.

## Don't Forget Seeds

Don't forget that many seeds are really very decorative. I have made pictures and collages from them, using both seeds bought in packets and others rescued from garden plants. For example, I wash melon seeds and dry them in the kitchen, finding them attractive enough to fashion flowers from their pale cream petal-like shapes, making the centres from small dried black and brown sunflower centres. Handsome kitchen calendars can be made from wide sky-blue sticky tape sold for sticking carpets together. Taken over a large brass curtain ring at the top for hanging, and with a paper calendar at the bottom, there is plenty of room for making melon seed flowers and buds with curving stems of string. Other seeds can be used in equally imaginative ways.

I often use lentils to cover the mechanics of a preserved arrangement in tawny colourings, the effect can be gay and unusual over a pinholder in a shallow dish. Being plant material, they can be confidently used for show designs. I once saw pearl barley used to make the path from cross to tomb in an Easter garden in church. When ideas start to flow for using run-of-the-mill culinary items for decoration the interest quickens. For instance, you can use cloves (the dried flower buds of the clove tree), peppercorns of black or white, cherry stones, and avocado stones. And why

*A cone is a useful base for an exotic made-up 'flower'.*

*Attractive calendars can be made from seeds and string.*

II

not use hairy brown coconuts decoratively for splendid large designs? Their shaggy shapes must surely add something not only amusing but also fantastic to a grouping.

Have you ever thought as you were buying millet for a swinging budgerigar that it is really quite decorative and could be used in a cascade over the front of a container? Sunflower seed comes in black, brown, and white humbug shapes, and maize for chicken feed is decorative too—all these things are plant material sold ready preserved. So why not use them? Large seeds are often seen stuck all round suitably shaped centres in imported 'made-up' flowers. As flower-like shapes these are acceptable as plant material in competitive work at shows judged according to the National Association of Flower Arrangement Societies' *Handbook of Schedule Definitions*.

# Doing What Comes Naturally

How do you set about preserving fresh plant materials so that their beauty goes on and on and on? There are a number of excellent ways. Some are useful for one kind of material, some for others. In the following pages I will cover all the easiest and most practical ways, from the traditional to the latest methods. Although as one Victorian book on preservation says: 'Mrs Experience is the best teacher', a little know-how can aid along the way and help you avoid early disappointments.

Most modern systems, as in the past, involve speed drying. In fact, when the plant forms are to be dried, the more quickly one can extract the moisture from living cells the better the results. Sometimes we can dry things naturally *in situ* in an arrangement, enjoying the design as the items gently preserve themselves. Other subjects will preserve themselves on the plant as it completes its life cycle out in the sun and fresh air. But the very best, tip-top results will more often be won under more controlled conditions indoors, where plant life of all seasons is dried at top speed, often employing an artificial drying medium or desiccant.

I do urge you to make things easy for yourself right from the beginning. Try to work along with Nature and your preserving will be all the more successful. If possible, anything destined for drying should be gathered on a warm, or at any rate dry, day, when foliage and petal are free from any form of outside moisture in the way of fog, dew, mist, or more obviously rain, or when the plants have been recently watered. We are aiming to *extract* moisture, and are halfway there if everything is dry to the touch to begin with. In a rain-lashed climate it may be somewhat tricky to find sufficient whole days that are the ideal—bone dry—but rain does ease off from time to time. Even in a very prolonged bad spell the atmosphere mops up a little because a breeze gets going, walls and pavements free themselves of moisture, and so do all but the most intricately petalled flowers. Then we are able to gather our material. The weather can change sufficiently for our purpose quite quickly, and it is amazing how good a weather prophet you become as you interest yourself in this hobby. As I say, I find garden walls and paths make good indicators, as does a teacloth drying on a line!

If you put damp subjects into any of the drying mediums (which I will describe later) these extract the excessive moisture and themselves quickly become over-charged with it, ceasing to function perfectly as they should. I have seen beginners trying to work with moist, clogged-up sand etc., and wondering why their preserved materials subsequently lost colour. Others find themselves constantly needing to reactivate the drying medium. This is such a fag, and can certainly be avoided.

## Cutting Material for Drying

When cutting for a fresh flower decoration it is advisable to do so in the cool, early part of the day or in the evening when the air is nearly always cooler and inclined towards moisture; the material is crisp and super-charged with sap at these times. Such cut material will stand well in water and enjoy a good life span indoors, particularly if, after gathering, the stems are provided with a long pre-arrangement drink in a bucket of water. For our purpose exactly the opposite applies, except for preservation by Method 2 (the glycerine method, described later). I have explained about picking in dry atmospheric conditions, and in the normal course of events there is no good reason for giving your material a drink before preserving it. If, however, you are offered some treasure from a friend's garden in the pouring rain it may be inopportune to turn it down—a desirable flower in the hand is worth a dozen promises! If you really must pick in unfortunate weather conditions, shake the flowers lightly when you get them indoors to remove excess water from petal and leaf surfaces, and leave in a jug or large jar, without water, for perhaps half an hour until surface moisture has completely dried out, and then preserve. As you see, it is really a matter of watching and waiting and then striking when the plant material is at exactly the right state.

Ideally, do not pick flagging flowers. If you are given something really special, on a very warm day perhaps, and it has wilted by the time you get it home, or if you buy a bunch of slightly wilted early 'shop' anemones or roses, revive them by standing the stem ends in a shallow drink of boiling water. When the flowers perk up, dry the stems, cut off any squashy sections, and preserve.

If I have picked a quantity of flower *heads* for making pictures and cannot get on with their preservation for a few hours, I find they stay crisp and unharmed if put into a plastic box with a snap-on lid, or tied in a roomy blown-up plastic bag and left until needed for preservation. But do not overcrowd such a box or bag. Flowers and leaves in bulk are surprisingly heavy and lower blossoms can get badly crushed by the weight of others on top. Do not preserve bruised flowers. On one or two occasions I have not been able to preserve until the following day but, as I always leave my boxes and bags in a dark cool spot, the contents were still in excellent form and still right for preserving.

**In frosty weather** Gathering in frosty weather may be necessary for such flowers as hellebores and winter jasmine, *Jasminum nudiflorum*. Before poor weather sets in, a protective cloche can be put into position over many early-blooming subjects. I always protect hellebores, anyway, to get undamaged blooms. Hellebores of all kinds preserve superbly; in prolonged frosts, however, the plant is starved of moisture, the flower heads and stems flop over as if suffering long summer drought; the petals (actually sepals) flag and it is difficult to achieve a good bold preserved shape until the weather eases up when, with luck, the whole stem and head pick up again. If you have forgotten to protect the plants from frost but you must preserve under these conditions, wilted flowers can be revived by the boiling water method mentioned earlier. Such flowers as winter jasmine can be picked in bud from the frosty garden and preserved after they have opened in water indoors.

**When to cut material** For preserving, every flower, leaf, berry or seedhead must be at its peak of perfection, whatever method you may be applying.

FLOWERS Every stamen should be standing firm, upright, separate, and intact. Petals must be crisp, unflagging, and unblemished. Their colours should be clear and unfaded by rain or long days of full sunlight. Their stems should squeak with health! Any flower even slightly past its best should be left where it is, unpicked.

FOLIAGE Firm and dry to the touch, unspotted, uneaten, not wind-torn or flagging. It should be showing good natural colour. Foliage can be immature or elderly, unless the glycerine method (Method 2) is chosen, when very young sprays of leaves, or those turning colour in the autumn, should be avoided.

## What Causes Failures?

In practice, some items are more successful than others. Sometimes, for no reason that you can see, one subject among its utterly successful and apparently identical companions, will not preserve, or else it preserves poorly; the whole branch will flop or the colour of a flower fade very rapidly. This is generally something to do with the weather conditions at the time of picking, or hidden disease, or overcrowding of the bunches or preserving boxes, damp preserving powders, or simply some jinx which affects pigments or preserving stability. It may happen one season and then not occur again. I cannot over-emphasise the point that it is too much to ask a rose, or anything else for that matter, to look good in the garden for three or four days and then, when it is slightly blurring round the edges, attempt its perfect preservation. When bees have been working over the flowers, the blooms will quickly deteriorate. Centres of flowers can, however, be pretty enough to preserve when the petals have recently dropped, and will give additional interest to many an unusual little design. Generally speaking, however, one just cannot have the best of two worlds. The chosen material is either destined to be enjoyed now, in the garden, or to be preserved for future enjoyment.

## Method 1 *Doing What Comes Naturally*

Some plant forms of good colour, texture, and shape, dry out and preserve themselves in a pleasing manner all on their own out in the garden, by a local pool, in a wood or recreation ground, or by the roadside. Even an unobservant eye can train itself to spot such items, although there is a funny weakness in the human intellect which suggests that anything which is free and easily available cannot be up to much! But flower arrangers have long appreciated that something beautiful can come from a farm ditch or the vegetable garden, and does not *have* to be a pretty flower. Be aware of beauty in all things. It can come quite unexpectedly in the form of a splendid sculptured seedhead, a handsome fungus, a glorious piece of well-mossed wood, a section of ridged bark, a delicate bract, or any one of a thousand bits and bobs to 'go' with flowers or even stand in for them when flowers are in short supply.

Every year arrangers in cold climates spend much money buying exotic foreign plant materials, often ignoring items of reasonably exotic appearance on their own home ground. I was made really aware of this last autumn when I was taking down the runner bean vines from their poles. I was about to throw away a few old dried bean pods I did not want for seed when I looked again and saw that I was handling some extremely attractive shapes, brown-black dappled with cream and lined with pure silver! These have since made ideal additions to mounted swags of dried materials, but would have been equally nice in arrangement for their texture and very unusual, foreign-looking appearance.

Many ordinary seedheads will dry out on the plant during spells of good weather, especially late in the season. They should be picked at perfection, in dry weather, and stored in boxes of suitable size, or arranged at once if you like, though if being used with fresh flowers they may require the bottoms of their stems to be painted with clear varnish, or dipped in melted wax, to prevent rotting. If you leave them over-long on the plants adverse weather may spoil the colour, set up mould, and start disintegration.

Seedheads do not only occur in autumn, however. In late spring and summer, do watch out for the delightful green (later turning cream then soft buff) seedheads of bluebell (endymion), grape hyacinth (muscari), scilla, agapanthus, fritillary, galtonia, tulip, and iris. Pick them at all colour stages, though when green they must be preserved by hanging (Method 7). The seedheads are often far longer in the stem than were the flowers of small subjects, and late last year I specially enjoyed working with cream-coloured seed sprays of grape hyacinth. These created a perfect setting for preserved orange-red strawberry foliage and small apricot dahlias. Other bulb and corm flowers give late offerings in wide variety, and I am particularly thinking of the seed cases of allium, gladioli, anemones, lilies, and such. Though keen gardeners may not agree to allow their best treasures to go to seed, as this can weaken a not-very-robust bulb or corm, and perhaps to some extent curtail next year's flowering, the occasional plants may be missed when faded flower sprays are being cut away; a holiday may intervene, or the bulbs be so prolific anyway that no-one bothers to dead-head them. So they produce seedheads for us to delight in, either picked at their green stage and dried by hanging indoors, or when they have shed their seed a little later on and have begun to dry out on the plants. And many a good seedhead has been rescued from the bonfire! If gathering those with seeds still left in them, shake the seeds out on a spare section of border–they can cause a terrible gritty trail indoors and disaster inside a framed picture. Should the season be too late for sure germination, put the seeds into a screw-top jar in the refrigerator until spring, when they may be sown in the usual manner. This is a good way of building up one's private stock of many things which provide fine seedheads. Some seeds, indeed many seeds, are visually attractive in themselves, and may be useful for collage making. Grape hyacinth seeds, for example, are jet black and most appealing.

A number of rock plants provide intensely beautiful seedheads, lovely for miniature work, which preserve themselves. I do specially urge you to gather a few sprays of the tiny silvery tissue-thin alyssum heads. These enchant me every year, cascading over a friend's wall like baby honesty (lunaria) pods and, like honesty pods, the fragile centres often disappear,

leaving behind dozens of miniature lorgnette shapes. As summer comes into its own, watch out for clematis seedheads and poppy 'pepper-pots', peony pods and all kinds of cones.

**Cones are so useful** Cones come in a wide range of sizes and are ever-useful for autumn flower-pieces and with nuts, fruits, and leaves for Grinling Gibbons' style swags and Christmas garlands. They can be sawn straight across to make 'roses' and, lightly frosted with packet frost at Christmas, they are intensely pleasing. The town in which I live has a castle, and the road on which the castle stands has houses of perfect Georgian architecture. At Christmas many of the lovely old doors carry home-made swags and these so often include cones. One year I specially admired on a door of soft mustard yellow a design which included very long and slender pale tan cones, lightly gilded and tied with a big, soft green bow. Larch cones in winter preserve themselves on long gently-curving branches. Cones can be stuck with small, gaily coloured preserved flowers and then swung like fairground boats, at different heights, on nylon fishing lines, from wire, to make delightful hanging mobiles which move in every lift of air.

Acorns are a must in my life for pictures and small swags, the 'saucers' making very naturalistic-looking homes for tiny empty snail shells stuck inside. In early autumn I fill my pockets with fat hoards of both 'cups' and 'saucers' as I walk my dog. After a stormy

*Pine cones used to make a delightful mobile.*

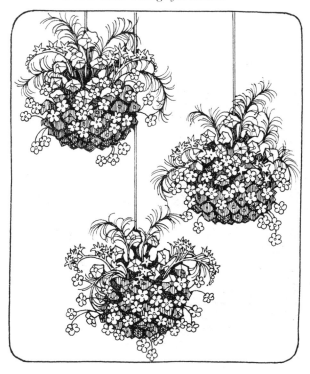

night I come home bearing small branches broken off the trees; these often carry very tiny acorns which give additional interest to calendars. Beech mast and the minute drumstick fruits of lime trees make other intriguing additions to my pocket collections.

Obviously one does not take the seedheads of rare wild flowers, but many quite common ones have a fine beauty. Knapweeds (centaurea) are common plants in many country areas. Leave them until the old, matted-looking flower petals can be pulled out in one piece to reveal inner creamy stars which are very flower like. Seedheads of wild vetches make other additions to small flower designs and can be collected while they are still tightly shut or when they have opened and discarded their seeds. At this last stage they twist and curl in a fascinating manner. Seedheads of wild umbelliferous subjects, cow parsley, water parsnip, hogweed etc., are available for gathering right up to Christmas, when they can be spangled attractively with silver 'frost' and packet 'snow'. Penny cress is a treasure and can be found growing sometimes where ground has been disturbed for road construction and so on.

**Garden seedheads and flowers** In the garden, do grow dictamnus, the burning bush, a perennial which

*In a container which is made from natural horn, lovely cream-coloured seedheads of grape hyacinth (Method 1) accompany helichrysum on mock stems, and beech preserved in glycerine. If the centres of helichrysum fluff, scoop them out to reveal a more interesting patterning.*

is lovely in seed, presenting glorious spires of eye-catching stars, purple-stained-brown, lined with pale corn colour; hellebores with their distinctive seed-heads which dry on the plant eventually like strange brown flowers; and iris for seedheads like small silver-grey lilies. Then there are angelica and fennel (pick them before they actually drop seed or you will have them setting up home all over the place), perennial poppies, astilbe, garden meadowsweet (fili-pendula), delphinium, hosta, primula, mallow, sea kale (crambe), red hot poker (kniphofia), phlomis, incarvillea and montbretia, just a few of the wide range of plants with super seedheads which either dry on the plant or can be gathered and dried quickly and without fuss by hanging indoors (Method 7).

Among garden flowers which dry themselves is anaphalis; this gives tiny white daisy-like flowers which are perfectly invaluable for use in small clusters or individually for petite designs. This is among the few white flowers which after cutting really do stay a good white, if not quite detergent-advertisement white. Pick the heads in bud, and open flower, on a dry day, and you can use them at once. Any which have matured a little and begun to make small powder-puffs in the centre can have these gently scratched away with your thumbnail to expose the soft green under centres. Mature ones will be brown in the middle, but give variety. All are invaluable for calendars and pictures.

**Popular everlasting flowers** Such everlasting flowers as helipterum, statice, xeranthemum, carlina, ammobium and rhodanthe, you may perhaps expect to find listed here under the 'dry themselves on the plant' category. Actually, far better results are achieved if they are harvested daily, when some are in bud, some just about to open, or having only just opened. They should be preserved according to Method 7 (by hanging). Do not wait until you can see the gold of their eyes, in those which have eyes, before picking them, or you will tend to get a flyaway tilting backwards of the petals in some subjects, and in others shaggy and rather scruffy-looking middles, and in all the colour may well be below par. Every year I get dozens of letters from readers of a well-known British garden journal querying such disappointments.

Many annuals give us the bonus of a good seedhead after the flower. I invariably pull up the whole plant, cut off the root, and there I have it. Good things include Shirley, Iceland, and other poppies; so many shapes and sizes, from slim jobs to more shapely, fatter pepper-pots. As with all garden seedheads, for variation of colour pick some 'in the green', some just turning colour, and others which have quite dried out. Preserve the first two stages by hanging. Clarkia, eschscholzia, candytuft (iberis), and love-in-a-mist (nigella) are all extremely pretty in seed.

From the vegetable garden I gather the grass-like

male section of sweet corn when this has dried out on the plant after doing its work. This is a good shape and a useful toast colour.

Other suitable seedhead subjects, this time from shrubs, include *Dorycnium suffruticosum*, which has dear little pink and white pea flowers followed by wooden stars in a range of colours which includes chocolate brown (from milk to plain). Pick them and use them in preserved arrangements straight away. Tiny brown wood 'flowers' also occur on the daisy bush (olearia), which grows easily from a cutting, incidentally. *Buddleia davidii* produces nice warm brown seed spikes, while magnolia, mahonia, peony, rhododendron, and *Cotinus coggygria* are other delights.

**Foliage which preserves itself** Some leaves also kindly preserve themselves and are ours just for the picking. I am thinking in particular of those spready, hardy bamboos. The leaves, gathered fresh, are any flower arranger's headache. They curl up on themselves and refuse to take water. They may, however, be preserved by ironing (Method 3), and then pressing flat for a day or two. But searching around under an established clump of plants will often yield ancient leaves which have preserved themselves, having kept their shape and turned a soft buff colour, sometimes dappled with strange blue-greens, Chinese red, and sable brown. Such leaves last indefinitely, adding a good pointed shape to many an arrangement. They may, of course, be painted or sprayed to any desirable colour. Search similarly under elderly magnolia bushes for their fallen leaves, like old very well-polished tooled leather, and under pampas grass (cortaderia) clumps, where curly bits, like wood shavings, dry themselves.

At summer's end, crocosmia and montbretia leaves turn to a rich sandy-brown colour and may be gathered on a dry day and used at once in arrangement, where their pointed, deeply ridged shapes are decorative enough even to stand alone in a modern arrangement. There are other leaves which dry themselves off perfectly on plant or shrub, sometimes when for some reason a branch has been damaged and slowly dies. If such items appeal to you, gather them happily–it is a fairly rare event nowadays to get something handsome for absolutely nothing!

**The Magic of Steaming**

Have you ever steamed an old hat to refresh it and restore its shape in the steam from a kettle? Preserved foliage which has become flat or crumpled in storing can be held over a steaming kettle and it will move back into its original shape, and creases will usually come out. Some leaves will change colour in the heat but may be even prettier than before. If you wish to change the shape of a large, preserved leaf, hold it in steam and, while it is still pliable, bend, curl, or twist it smoothly to a new shape. Preserved dock, mimosa,

statice, astilbe, and other subjects which have become crushed may be gently shaken in the steam of a kettle and the shapes will be magically restored.

Thin dried stems of wisteria, honeysuckle (lonicera), broom (cytisus), and slim pieces of burnt gorse (ulex), can be re-shaped to curving shapes in the same way. Hold or tie the shape in position until the item cools. Ferns may also be re-shaped this way.

# More Ways to Success

**Method 2**   *The Glycerine Method*
So far as I have been able to discover, foliage and seedheads have been preserved in glycerine and water mixtures only in comparatively recent years. None in my collection of early flower arranging books says anything about this method at all. As it is so very easy and simple, the idea that it is only a recent discovery surprises me, for most items so treated last practically for ever and retain pliable stems and leaves, unlike material preserved by those methods which involve drying. There are colour changes, but these are always lovely, adding variety and something a little off-beat to an arrangement. Leaf colour can change to cream, coffee, glossy boot-polish brown, green-brown, blue-green, or near to yellow. Beech, for example, that most popular foliage for preserving by this method, will vary in colour from rich chocolate to bronze-green, depending on the time of year and the length of time it is left in the mixture. Other foliages which colour attractively are magnolia, ivy (trails and berries), privet (ligustrum), cotoneaster in berry, box (buxus), whitebeam (sorbus), magnolia, choisya, while sprays of conifer give lightness to many an outline and variety of shape to a design of foliage only. Eucalyptus of various sorts preserves nicely, and if you add a little red ink to the preservative mix in summer a warm pink staining is usually assured. Pussy willow will hang on to its 'pussies' for many a year, and stephanandra holds every graded leaf. Sweet corn foliage preserves like long silk ribbons. Corkscrew hazel (*Corylus avellana contorta*) and whirligig willow (*Salix tortuosa*), should be preserved before they leaf up, or the twirling oddness of their appeal is lost under heavy foliage; if the corkscrew hazel carries catkins or nuts these will stay intact. Azalea, before it starts to colour in autumn, makes a pleasant

*A favourite small figurine group, made entirely from sweet corn husks, sets out on a flower gathering expedition among golden narcissus, polyanthus and* Mahonia japonica, *under a tree of heavily lichened thorn and lamb's tail catkins. This very long-lasting scene is completely preserved. It includes shell-like fungus and bright mosses.*

subject, as do pieris, elaeagnus, berberis, rose, viburnum, and many more. Before any foliage subject is introduced to the glycerine treatment, very straight stems may be eased into curves in the warmth of the hand to bring a feeling of life to subsequent designs.

Before attempting to preserve sprays and branches, go over them carefully and trim away excess side shoots and leaves which are imperfect, and scrape and split open the stem ends.

**The glycerine solution** The mixture is made up of one part glycerine to two parts boiling water. The boiling water is necessary to facilitate the intake of the solution. Stir the mixture well and use hot. Some people add a handful of salt or a quarter-teaspoonful of a mild antiseptic to the mix to prevent mould, but you should have no trouble with mould if you treat and store your leaves indoors, in the dry. Left-over mixture may be used again, even if discoloured. It must, however, be re-boiled and used hot.

Stand the stem ends in the mixture, two or three inches deep. It is not necessary to have too great a depth, though the level must be kept topped up should the mixture be drunk dry! Very thick leaves should be rubbed over with a cloth soaked in the mixture before and during processing. Preservation takes from a few days to a month, depending on the subject and the colour desired. For variation of colour remove some leaves before they have completely changed colour. Normally, the foliage is 'done' when the veins on the underside of the leaves are seen to have completely absorbed the glycerine mix. If left over-long, small globules of glycerine will appear on the foliage, but these can be washed away by swishing the branches briefly through a bowl of soapy water, or water with washing-up liquid in it. Then allow the foliage to dry naturally. Foliage must not be picked too young or it will not 'take'. Smooth leaves are easier to preserve by this method than rough ones. If immature leaves on top of a spray refuse to preserve, it is easy enough to cut them away neatly. Midsummer is a good time to preserve deciduous subjects, but do not be a slave to this. Evergreens of all kinds can be preserved, when convenient, at practically any time, except when new growth is being made. I have found that liquidambar (the sweet gum) glycerines to a red colour if picked and treated when it has just turned colour in autumn. But on the whole treat foliage before it changes colour, as the colour change is a sign that the material will not now draw in the glycerine drink. A copper hue can be achieved in green beech and other foliage by dissolving a little permanganate of potash in the hot solution.

Do experiment for yourself. Try out any well-shaped leaf. If you have no garden, have a go with the leaves of pot plants—many, such as ficus, grevillea, aspidistra, preserve excellently this way. Failure rarely occurs, though one spray in a batch may, for some inexplicable reason, not 'take'.

*This refreshing design for a spring morning has beech leaves preserved in glycerine, curls of hot-spot-dried montbretia foliage, driftwood and pot plant cyclamen leaves and daffodils dried in a desiccant.*

Preserve what is to hand. Seedheads of many kinds do well and keep their fruits intact. Try *Iris foetidissima*, dock, clematis, old man's beard (wild clematis), cow parsley, sycamore, beech complete with seed mast, chestnut, and lime. Border seedheads, like hosta, lily, and montbretia, should not be overlooked. The odd slight smell of musty cupboards assumed by subjects treated with glycerine is to my mind the only unattractive element in this means of preservation. Anti-freeze can be used in place of glycerine, but I have always found glycerine to be more successful. Some people add cake colourings or green ink to hot solutions of glycerine or anti-freeze to assure a bright green colour.

**Floating foliage in the mixture** Some subjects such as ferns will be found to preserve better if actually submerged in the glycerine solution. Bergenia, hosta, trails of ivy, lily-of-the-valley, and violet foliage are specially recommended. A piece of crumpled tinfoil placed on top will keep the foliage submerged. When the leaves change colour, remove them and mop off excess solution with tissues, then dry out on blotting paper. Some leaves stay a good bright green after immersion. Such foliage as ficus (rubber plant) can be either stood in glycerine, or if stemless it should be floated in the solution.

*Handsome, orange-berried* Iris foetidissima, *with preserved leaves which were pinned into swirling shapes before drying (Method 7). The curled foliage gives spirit and an impression of movement to the overall design.*

**Points to note** Leaves of *Fatsia japonica,* so useful to the arranger, tend to flop when preserved by standing their stems in the solution, unless you give them a slim stick to support them. Bind or tape the stick into position. Or you can make a stitch with florist's wire through the middle part of the main rib from the back, then twist both ends of wire down the stem as a support.

I have found it more successful to preserve individual leaves rather than whole large rosettes of rhododendron, standing the small individual stems in the solution. Sprays of rose foliage 'do' very well, holding on to any heps, which stay fat and pleasing. *Rosa rubrifolia* all set with fruits is a special attraction. The herb of grace (*Ruta* Jackman's Blue) changes to a delicate pale biscuit colour, its neat little filigree leaf shapes being extremely pretty.

Glycerined foliage may be arranged with other preserved subjects out of water or introduced into fresh flower and foliage groups, to the advantage of both. When used in water, with fresh plant material, the ends of glycerined items should be painted over with nail varnish, picture varnish, or treated with candle wax; all these prevent mildew.

**Bleaching leaves and seedheads** You might like to try bleaching some of the foliage during or after pre-serving it, to give gradations of colour and extra zing to a design. To do this, stand some of the stems in a sunny window or a greenhouse as you preserve them, and they will slowly go paler in colour. Of course, in very warm situations one must closely watch the level of the glycerine, as it tends to evaporate while you are not looking! Conditions must not be so hot that the leaves preserve by *drying*. If, after it has been preserved, you wish foliage to have a softer, creamy-parchment, or paler brown colour you can try laying the branches out of doors during sunny spells, but it is best to bring them indoors again before the dew falls.

**Storing subjects preserved in glycerine** Storing glycerined foliage is simple, for it can be kept anywhere which is not actively damp. It will not re-absorb moisture from the air and spoil, as does material dried in desiccants, but moulds will form naturally if the leaves are left oily with glycerine, or if kept over-long in damp places. Store material in boxes and plastic bags. Individual leaves can be stored flat, one on top of another. Boxes under a spare bed, up in a dry attic, or in the cupboard under the stairs, make good storage. Mothballs placed in with the material deter insects. Dusty leaves can be flicked through water containing washing-up liquid and then dried.

**Flowers preserved in glycerine** Long sprays of lime with flowers and bracts will take the glycerine mix, but first strip away a great deal of the foliage. *Garrya elliptica* (the silk tassel bush) when preserved by this method gives more pliable results than when the swinging flowers are preserved by drying. This, too, is the best method of preserving *Molucella laevis* (bells of Ireland), and other firm flowers and bracts you can treat are eryngium (sea holly), hydrangea, and many more. There will, however, be changes of colour. If heather is glycerined for three days it will keep its natural colour and all its flower bells. Leave it longer, and you will get browning.

*A stick is a useful support for a floppy leaf.*

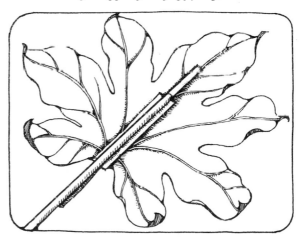

RIGHT
*If her bouquet is made of
suitable flowers a brides-
maid can preserve it to
remind her of the occasion.
This one was made of
roses, delphinium and
gentian. The foliage is
box, cyclamen and
elaeagnus. After
preservation the bouquet
was sprayed with clear
polyurethane varnish to
give it a porcelain flower
finish.*

OPPOSITE PAGE
*All on a summer's day;
the flowers of early spring
and summer come together
in a glass jar which has a
lid, to carry their beauty
into the flower-starved
days of winter.*

20

**Method 3** *Preserving by Ironing*

Individual leaves and grasses can be quickly and simply preserved for future arrangements by ironing them! I prefer ironing to pressing leaves between newspapers under the carpet, for my own attempts at the latter always led to many broken leaves. Ironed foliage keeps excellent colour, and autumn-tinted leaves particularly so. The fabulous tints are more or less exactly retained. First cover your ironing board with an old sheet, for even country-grown leaves are surprisingly dirty. Then, with a hot iron, press firmly over the leaves on both sides until they are crisp, taking the greatest care not to cause damage to the main ribs. The smell is pretty frightful, so do keep a window open. After ironing leave the foliage for a few days under a number of heavy books then, handling carefully, for the leaves are very brittle, either store them in stacks of all one kind together in plastic bags, or arrange them at once. Virginia creeper in autumn is superb, and the graded leaves may be stuck individually to a suitable branch for a very realistic effect. A slightly more involved method is to dip individual leaves in melted paraffin wax, then iron between newspaper.

**Method 4** *Skeletonising Foliage*

A skeletonised leaf is one in which all the leaf except the main ribs and the delicate intricate network of intersecting veins is missing. Available commercially are skeletonised magnolia, poplar, and a few other nice shapes. You can skeletonise your own. In a large pan of water boil up half a small packet of powder detergent and put the foliage in carefully. Boil for half an hour. You are not cooking cabbage, so do only a very few leaves at a time, depending on their size and the size of the pan. Some people let the leaves stay in the solution until it is cold and then strip away the slimy green leaf tissue. Others remove the foliage from the hot mixture, run cold water over it, and strip it at once. Leave the skeletonised leaves in a solution of household bleach until they are creamy-white. You can colour them now if you wish, using a hot water dye. For brighter colours spray with aerosol car-body paints. Slowly dry, then press flat, or roll them round a pencil to make pretty curls. There is yet another method of skeletonising leaves, which is to boil them in a teaspoonful of soda with a quart of water for about an hour. Leave them in the mix to cool, and then scrape as before.

**Method 5** *Old English Pot-pourri*

To make a dry pot-pourri, so much admired in the past but nowadays rarely seen outside the private sitting rooms of stately homes, or sold in expensive boxes and special china balls in the large stores, is a pleasant occupation for a summer day. It is also a good way of using up those broken petals from your pre-

served fatalities! There are many old recipes, but the following is my own favourite. On a dry day gather a bowlful of lavender flowers, red rose and marigold petals, leaves of bay, marjoram, rosemary, lemon thyme, mint, balm, or indeed anything which smells nice. Dry thoroughly on newspapers in a warm place, and add dried and pulverised orange rind, lemon peel, with about a teaspoonful of allspice, half an ounce of ground cloves, and a little orris root. And there you are, such a mixture nicely blended to suit your own taste will charm you and be far removed from the Eastern bazaar perfumes of some of the commercial products. Sprinkle on top dried, colourful flower petals or tiny, whole preserved flower heads. Make up into bags, beribboned for hanging, put into bowls, or box in transparent boxes tied with satin or velvet ribbons.

**Method 6** *Crystallising Flowers*

The traditional iced cake is the natural focal point of birthday and Christmas parties, weddings and christenings. You can create unusual and extremely attractive cake decorations by crystallising fresh flowers. Any flower with a sweet scent is edible, and flowers which have been crystallised may be kept for years in boxes or tins with air holes in the lids if stored in a very dry cupboard.

Forget-me-nots and pansies, roses and sprigs of heather, primroses, and delphinium pips (buds) are coloured with cake colouring suitable to the flowers. Mix together two parts caster sugar to one part granulated sugar on a saucer and add drops of the colouring. Crush with a spoon, and put through a sieve to remove lumps. Mix three to four teaspoonfuls of rose-water to one of powdered gum arabic and paint the front and back of each flower with this, supporting the flower with your hand as you go. Don't be too heavy-handed with the solution. While still wet, sprinkle both sides with the sugar mixture. Leave to dry out on a wire cake-cooling tray for about a week.

# *Home and Dry!*

**Method 7** *Drying by Hanging*

I think that drying by hanging sounds rather ghoulish when written, but this method of preservation of plant material is one of the oldest. For goodness knows how many years, women in temperate climates have tied lavender, teasels, bulrushes, statice, achillea, pampas, iris seedheads, Chinese lanterns, etc., into trim bunches with string or twine and hung them indoors, high on old beams and rafters, to dry off. It was, and is, generally those subjects of an obviously 'everlasting' kind which proved most successful. The true secret of keeping the best colour lies in very quick preservation. Today the best place for hanging flowers is the airing cupboard, where small bunches will dry within a few days. A kitchen, though warm, is not perhaps a good place to choose, because of the risk of steam, unless it has a very good constant source of heat such as a boiler.

Many people use a shed or the garage, but these too are not particularly good. Although the general advice is to select somewhere dark and airy, airiness is not really necessary so long as the bunches are kept small and conditions are conducive to speedy drying. Sheds and garages though often dark, which is good for keeping colour, are inclined to be cool and moist. Such conditions tend towards encouraging mildew and discolouration. Another thing I find is that one is likely to forget the things drying out there. The tool-shed at the end of autumn, for example, will probably not be visited very regularly, unless you're a keen gardener. I know a flower arranger in a tiny single-storey cottage who each season manages to preserve an impressive number of things simply by hanging them in bunches all along the arms of wire coat hangers. She hangs these up in her bedroom over the central heating radiators until the material is crisp and dry to the touch and the stems firm. A greenhouse may be the ideal in many respects except that important one of bright light destroying good colour.

It is best, immediately after drying, for the bunches to be taken down and stored carefully away in boxes or clear plastic bags in a dry place in the house, or arranged straightaway into containers. Because this method is so very easy, costs nothing but time, and has perhaps a 99 per cent. success rate, the same combinations of flowers have appeared in dried groups for generations, and still do, more often than not unimaginatively arranged in, at best a copper jug, at worst a cut glass vase. And so in theory we are utterly tired of them. In fact, all these old favourites are still preserved each year by even the keenest arrangers, but they arrange them in far more arresting ways than in the past. There are few people nowadays who would go into their friends' homes and fall about with admiration at, say, a bowl of mixed statice, however wide the range of colour. On the other hand, a well-designed flower-piece of pale yellow to soft apricot statice, in association with small toning autumn leaves, and pompon dahlias, with perhaps a figurine in blending colours, would be imaginative and would catch the eye, especially if it stood on a softly polished base. There are hosts of really exciting and even off-beat ways to use traditionally dried flowers.

**Material to dry by hanging** Small double roses, lavender, bulrushes, zinnias, achillea, larkspur, acanthus, protea, green and red tassels of love-lies-bleeding, allium, delphinium, anaphalis, cockscomb (celosia),

*Broom can be dried in curves by tying it in circles.*

*Artemisia ludoviciana*, small bunch-petalled chrysanthemums, crocosmia, eryngium, small double dahlias, and a number of other flowers, will usually dry off handsomely if hung, a few stems together, in the airing cupboard, immediately over the hot tank—though not actually touching it. Pussy willow preserves well, too, and some sprays I have treasured for years. It is an advantage to gently curve the stems before drying, as curving shapes are generally much more useful than straight ones. Pussy willow can be preserved also by the glycerine treatment (Method 2), and this is the best way if you are likely to handle the stems a great deal as the 'pussies', being less brittle, stay securely in place. Fresh green broom tied in circles and left in the airing cupboard to dry will preserve itself in useful, sweeping curves.

The proper name for bunting-bright orange-coloured Chinese lanterns, Cape gooseberry, winter cherry, etc., is physalis, though a little girl I know has her own name goblins' lamps. At any rate, this bright thing is an easily grown perennial to dry by hanging. Pick the long curving stems when the majority of swinging lantern-like seedheads show good colour; any still green will keep this colour for some considerable time, adding variety. Gather in good time before wet and frosts spoil them. If, after preserving, the lanterns get a bit squashed in store, they are easily inflated again if you gently blow through a tiny hole you can make at the pointed end. To give variation of form, some lanterns may be opened along the main ribs, so that they can be curled back into 'petals'. This exposes a small delight inside—an unexpected shiny orange berry. The bright colour of the physalis lasts for years, though if you like the

RIGHT
*A linear arrangement of cascading laburnum and clematis.*

OPPOSITE PAGE
*A birthday cake for a little girl's party decorated with a maypole design topped with a posy of buttercups, daisies, lilacs and pink May blossom. The cake itself has an edible decoration of crystallised lilac and daisies.*

*Chinese lanterns can be cut open to make 'flowers'.*

shape and the colour does not fit into your home colour scheme you can alter it by spray painting. Festive effects are possible at Christmas if you lightly spray the tangerine colour with gold or an off-beat mixture of silvery blue and ice green, and finally add the merest dash of sparkle. Then they become magic fruits indeed.

Honesty (lunaria) is another dear old favourite. A biennial, its seed pods preserve with ease, either by hanging, or when the stems are placed in a container to dry off. Pick at perfection and, after drying, spend an evening rubbing away the outer portions to expose the shining silver moons inside, or pick earlier when the outer part of the seed cases is showing grape-purple staining and dry by hanging; at this stage many arrangers find them particularly likeable. Honesty may be glycerined at this, its green-purple stage (Method 2). Re-sow some of the seed or you will find yourself honesty-less one day! Echinops, the globe thistle, will also dry by hanging. Pick before the flowers open for the best steel-blue colour.

The annual and hardy border centaureas give scaly bud-like forms before and after flowering. Usually a pretty tan brown, in *Centaurea pulchra major* the rustling heads are silver buff.

Among popular annuals to grow from seed to dry by hanging are ammobium, an 'everlasting' subject with white petals and domed yellow centres; *Helipterum grandiflorum*, giving crisp little straw-like flowers, double and semi-double in such nice variations of pink and cream; *Xeranthemum annuum*, which supplies strong upright stems topped with pink- and lavender-

coloured flowers; and don't forget *Rhodanthe rosea* on your seed list, for its pink flowers with gay yellow eyes, or choose a packet of mixed colours. Mixed statice is still grown by flower arrangers, today's seed houses producing colours in a particularly wide and attractive range. However, one of the best annuals for our purpose, to my mind, is *Statice suworowii*, the candlewick statice. A must for its richness of pink flower spikes, which make admirable additions to so many decorations. All these annuals should be carefully observed as they come to perfection, and I go up and down my borders gathering them daily, for as I have pointed out previously colour cannot be so clear and long-lasting if the flowers are even slightly past their best when picked.

Everlasting flowers such as helichrysum *will* dry by hanging but this way the stems do not usually preserve with sufficient strength to support the flower heads. It is really best if only heads are gathered, dried in the house face up on cake-cooling trays after being wired with false stems, or stuck to mock stems after drying. Pick only buds and just-ready-to-open flowers. Some, you will find, open prettily indoors, escaping the dingy grey-yellow centres you may expect from flowers which have been allowed to open naturally in the garden, where every passing insect is likely to alight, pollinating the flowers and so spoiling them for our purpose. Helichrysum quickly go drab looking, I find, if left in a chilly, slightly damp atmosphere, or a dusty one. The heads store attractively if heaped in a basket until needed, but colour keeps better in a lidded box. There are a thousand and one ways of using preserved everlasting flowers. Wire the heads and make them up into flower balls with ribbons (using a dry foam ball as a base), as flower 'trees' (using a dry foam cone shape with a dowel rod as trunk, cemented into a painted plant pot), or as decorations for calendars, pictures, collages, etc, as well as straightforward flower arrangements.

Molucella (bells of Ireland) defeats many arrangers, who endeavour to preserve it by the hanging method. Perhaps best of all if grown throughout in the greenhouse, it is most successfully preserved by the glycerine method (Method 2). It turns cream coloured but can be spray painted.

*Limonium bonduellii* is a sunshine-yellow annual which you might well like in your garden, along with annual poppy seedheads and love-in-a-mist (nigella), for its amusingly shaped and nicely coloured pods. All may be dried by hanging, as may the centres of many daisy flowers, such as the warm brown middles of annual chrysanthemums, smaller sunflowers, and the like. These can look eye-catching and off-beat in arrangements.

Delphiniums pink and delphiniums blue keep their colour remarkably well when hung to dry. The white ones tend to grey, and very palest baby-ribbon pink

*A dry foam cone provides the support for this 'tree'.*

and blue ones may fade in time, presenting a rather aged look. It is interesting that preserved delphiniums have been found in Egyptian tombs. Though over a thousand years old they were still incredibly blue when found. Although not quite so impressive as that, I have preserved ones arranged under glass in a picture which are still a fine true blue after 15 years. The best colour is retained by the deeper blues, rather than the soft sky colours, but it is astounding how these and forget-me-nots, as described later (Method 8), keep their fresh colouring exactly, perhaps longer than anything else I know. This is doubly surprising when the blue pigment in fabrics and paint is often not a good stayer.

Whole spikes of delphinium dry effectively by hanging them upside down on their long stems until all the blooms—and the *stems*—feel crisp to the touch. Pick when a good number of the lower florets have opened but before the bottom one has started to drop. Bring indoors and hang individual spikes in the airing cupboard. Small side sprays (laterals) prove equally effective when it comes to drying and are, of course, not so much missed from the garden display. Their stems dry off speedily, for the water content is not so high. There may be some slight crumpling of individual petals during drying but one can, with patience, smooth these out or even iron them carefully with a very cool iron—not so boring and tedious as it sounds, or so lengthy a process as all that unless you have a very large number of heads to do. Immature green laterals with their unopened buds will also dry most winningly. Absolute perfection, not only of del-

*Purely for fun! A dowel rod stem on a pinholder supports a round piece of foam into which are stuck dried sunflowers, their centres preserved by hanging upside down in the airing cupboard (Method 7), their petals dried separately in salt (Method 8), then stuck back into place! Thin iris leaves were preserved in the arrangement, being coaxed into curves as they dried.*

27

*Flowers preserved and then arranged in the Flemish style of flower painting. Such a design shows how it is possible to make up a posy of the flowers of the whole year. Here primroses, auricula, striped tulips and daisies rub shoulders with roses, poppy anemones, candytuft, wheat and berries.*

*Romantically arranged in a tiny china basket, the flowers of yesterday – grape hyacinth, periwinkle, pink candlewick statice, auricula, lavender, heart's ease (miniature viola), and forget-me-not seem in perfect harmony with a little Victorian book, The Language of Flowers.*

phinium colour but also of petal shape, is achieved by drying with desiccants (Method 8), which is particularly successful with individual florets large and small. Delphiniums give such a welcome touch of blue or pink to a preserved flower-piece, and that their shape is somewhat different from most other flowers we can preserve in this manner is another pointer to their excellence. Larkspur of every colour is another winner dried by hanging, as are grasses of all kinds. And do try *Stachys lanata* (lamb's ear).

And so, as we come towards the end of this chapter, you may imagine my airing cupboard at all times of the year is in use for many other things than airing linen. Indeed, it is often something of a mad riot of subjects in varying stages of preservation, with only

one shelf ever kept permanently for the job the architect intended. But I comfort myself with the fact that anyway it is not supposed to be a good thing to keep *fabrics* over-long in a hot cupboard! When drying plant forms in such a cupboard it is absolutely vital to keep it free from wet clothing or laundry, as one can so easily build up a steamy atmosphere to the detriment of the drying flowers. Then, either mould is set up, or the plant material takes too long over its preserving and so loses out on best colour and may, at worst, not preserve at all.

All the methods described so far are very simple and available to everyone. I was amused when I read in a Victorian flower book the directions for making up an airtight box for drying flowers such as del-

phiniums, asters, and roses. 'The simple instructions,' said the writer, 'have been supplied by one of the largest exporters of dried flowers in Germany. Every home has brimstone available,' the writer continued, going on to describe the method of smoking flowers inside a box by pushing a small bowl of burning brimstone through a hole left in the base. After this the blooms were plunged into a mixture which included nitric acid. That is what I would call a complicated hobby!

## Colouring and Bleaching

The other day I was offered on a market stall softly coloured honesty 'pennies' imported, said the sales lady, from Italy. I came home and dyed some of my own, far less expensively, with a dye from the chain store. The silver translucency of the honesty gleamed gently and most attractively through the pale pinks, blues, and lettuce-green dyes I had chosen. Preserved flowers which have lost colour, flowers and leaves whose colours you wish to alter, and seedheads and fruits can be sprayed with aerosol car paint so long as the plant material is not of too absorbent a texture. More delicate colours can be obtained by leaving plant material overnight floating submerged in a bowl of dye, and then drying again, or by touching up with water colour, oil paints, or even pastel chalks. When making up dye use boiling water and stir well. I recommend wearing rubber gloves!

Some leaves or seedheads one may prefer to see bleached cream or off-white, like many imported ones. Leave the dried material to have a good long soaking in undiluted household bleach until it has assumed the desired colour. Do not leave very fragile items overlong, however, or they will start to disintegrate. Plant forms such as teasels are tricky, perhaps, and it may be easiest to suspend the individual heads in jars of bleach, sticking the stems down through a lid of chicken wire. Driftwood may also be bleached in a bucket of bleach, or if you wish for a darker colour it can be stained. Often a rub over with some dark stain shoe polish is all that is required.

Oxblood stain polish gives a warm glow to dusty brown leaves and driftwood. Dark brown polish produces an effect of leather which has been tenderly cared for. Floor stains of various colours are useful to have in your flower cupboard for polishing stout leaves and for bringing up the subtle textures and grains in driftwood. Wood, and bleached leaves, may be coloured by rubbing food colourings, shoe dyes,

*Christmas, and dried stems of Queen Anne's lace lightly sprayed with 'snow' suggest the outline of a stable. On a black glass base, preserved freesia, iris leaves and ivy support a cherub peeping into a straw-filled manger. Scatterings of unpolished rice on the black base bring good visual balance to the design.*

or pastel crayons over them. Large leaves which look dull can be given a shine by rubbing them over gently with a rag soaked in light oil or a with a special leaf polish which you can buy for house plants. A friend of mine keeps her driftwood snow white by leaving it from time to time in her washing machine after taking out the laundry. Then she scrubs it and allows it to dry in the sun. Some foliage, such as aspidistra, will dry to a pleasant creamy colour if preserved in glycerine (Method 2) in a sunny window or a greenhouse.

Stripped bleached broom can be bought at florists' shops or it may be stripped at home by cooking it in a pressure cooker. Under a running tap the outer skin is then simply rubbed away, and the material finally bleached white. If dried by hanging, broom stays a soft green but becomes rather brittle; if glycerined it changes to a near black colour. Burnt gorse from heathland twists attractively, and though at first dirty to handle it lasts for years. Interesting bare shapes of ivy branch, wisteria, etc., can be peeled easily by boiling them in a solution of two teaspoonfuls of soda to two quarts of water. After further soaking, thin stems can often be re-shaped by gentle manipulation. It is worth remembering, too, that you can lighten the colours of nuts by giving them a soak in bleach, and that fresh magnolia and other leaves sometimes turn white if you boil them.

## Enamelling Leaves and Flowers

Small fresh fruits, flowers and leaves can be brushed over with two to three coats of enamel in a colour to match a room. Although the idea may be abhorrent to some of us, it must be admitted that white enamelled flowers are particularly pleasing. Enamelled flowers make unusual swags, calendars and frames for mirrors, as well as decorations for cakes (obviously not to be eaten) and arrangements of the more usual kind. The coats must be smoothly built up, allow each to dry before applying the next. Colouring in these ways is very much a matter of personal taste, and no one *has* to do it, but sensitively coloured and presented material can sometimes be most acceptable. As explained elsewhere, artificially coloured plant materials are now accepted by the National Association of Flower Arrangement Societies of Great Britain at shows judged according to their *Handbook of Schedule Definitions*, unless otherwise stated in any particular show schedule. It is doubtful, however, whether plant material which has been heavily enamelled would be always acceptable.

*Two perfectly preserved daffodils have been lightly sprayed with matt lacquer to strengthen their trumpets.*
*This gives a longer span of 'life' to such flowers. The arrangement shows the diverse and lovely colourings which can be achieved when preserving leaves by Method 2.*

# Everything But Perfume

**Method 8**  *Preserving with Desiccants*

Now we come to what I consider to be the most satisfactory method of preserving the majority of flowers, many leaves, and even seedheads. This is by speed drying in what are called desiccants or drying agents—substances such as borax, alum, silver sand, silica gel, or one of the named products on the market. These take moisture speedily from the plant material, drawing it into themselves. The great thing about preserving in a desiccant is that the contours of the plant or leaf are exactly retained, as in life, the natural colour being superbly captured so that it is hard to tell that the items are not freshly picked. Only the perfume is missing and any normal glossiness of petal texture in, say, a buttercup; but as you can give such a flower an artificial gloss this really matters little. Often the only way to tell at a glance whether a flower is dried or fresh lies in the fact that the stem of a subject dried in a desiccant will have shrunk slightly.

For this method of drying you require deep plastic or tin boxes with tight-fitting lids. The sizes will depend upon what you wish to preserve. Naturally you would get many flower *heads* into a tin which would not be large enough to take long stems—very long-stemmed flowers can be anchored on a pinholder in a deep tin or jar, such as a catering size coffee tin. The bottom of the box is covered with the desiccant, the depth of desiccant depending on the flowers, but from half an inch is sufficient. The blooms are placed on the desiccant, face up. Cosy them in by trickling more of the drying agent very carefully and gently around the petals, taking great care that the flower's natural contours are held. If you position a flower or leaf carelessly, with bent-back twisted petals, sadly, it will be a flower with bent-back, twisted petals which you eventually take out!

It is a good idea to gently support the petals in natural shapes with a cocktail stick, or your finger, as you pour on the desiccant, for it is important that all the contours are given support and every crevice between the petals is filled. When the flowers are covered you may add more layers of flowers and desiccant, but your final layer must be the drying agent. No piece of plant material should touch its neighbour, neither is it a very good idea to mix too great a selection of diverse subjects in the same tin, for then they will dry off at different rates. It is, for example, better to fill one box with zinnias, another with *Rosa rubrifolia* leaf sprays, for the latter will preserve more speedily than the former. If the two are mixed higgledy-piggledy, the resultant disturbance of the box as the quicker-drying items are removed is something that is better avoided.

*Positioning blooms in a container of desiccant.*

Of course, when you become more experienced you will develop a sixth sense as to just how long things will take to 'do', and it is possible to build up a box by placing quick-drying subjects towards the top and the slower ones nearer the bottom. Don't be frightened about this kind of thing, however; it does not really matter if, say, the rose leaves remain in the preserving powder longer than necessary whilst waiting for the zinnias to dry. They may be more brittle at first but will, in time, absorb a little moisture from the atmosphere and so become less susceptible to damage during handling and storage.

When the box is full, put on a tight-fitting lid. It is sometimes advised that the lid should be sealed with tape, but this is unnecessary. Now place the box in a warm dry place such as the shelf of an airing cupboard above the hot water tank. I have also left boxes of drying subjects on top of a radiator on *low heat*, and one friend has a shelf above her refrigerator, making use of the waste heat, whilst another places boxes above a hot air duct of the central heating system. Ideally, requirements are constant warmth and a dry atmosphere. Speed in drying is what matters. Two things to beware of are (1) over-fierce heat which might char delicate subjects, turning them toast brown and causing damage to petal and leaf structures; (2) over-cool and slightly moist conditions, which delay the drying process and lead to poor colour retention and even possible collapse of the plant cells.

**How long does it take?** Most flowers, leaves, etc. will be absolutely crisp to the touch in any length of time from a day or so up to two or three weeks, depending on the flower, the amount of heat, and the desiccant chosen. But thicker areas of material, such as stems and seed pods, the thick section at the back of many flower heads, juicy buds such as roses, and some leaves, will take a little longer than the flower itself. You must, however, leave the subject in the preserving agent until *all* parts feel completely dry to the touch. This is something you must not shirk! I sometimes remove flowers such as roses and carnations when the actual petals are dry but when either the stems or the calyces are still incompletely so, finishing off the process on top of a night storage radiator and protecting the flower petals from the heat with crumpled tissue paper, until all parts are completely dried. So do experiment for yourself with this, choosing your own hot spot but obviously taking precautions against any risk of overheating and accident. In no time at all you will come to recognise those flowers with which, having a special sturdiness about them, one can take liberties. Far more liberties can be taken with a rose in late summer, for example, than with a sweet pea in June, or at any other time for that matter. Before drying such flowers and bracts as euphorbia (poinsettia) and similar items known to drip latex from their cut stems, burn the stem ends after cutting.

When the flowers are dry in every part, remove them, with care, from the desiccant. Take particular care with the very slim-petalled ones; these will be paper-dry and temporarily very delicate. Gently shake or brush away any granules of preservative still adhering to the material. On no account dig into the preservative to extract the flowers, or you will surely do them harm. Small boxes are simple to tip out above your waiting left hand, allowing the drying medium to flow away through your fingers and on to a sheet of newspaper underneath. As they appear, the flowers are caught and then transferred to waiting storage boxes. Another method, when a large number of very small flower heads are being extracted with difficulty because of their smallness, is to shake the desiccant gently from the box into a large flour sieve. As the desiccant is softly shaken through the sieve odd bits of broken petal may be removed and thrown away and the flowers rescued and boxed individually. Yet another way, when preserving sturdy subjects, is to shake the box and preservative slowly from side to side; if it is carrying not too great a wealth of flowers these will move to the top, from where they can be extracted. If, however, the boxes are very deep, or too heavy, the whole thing can be very carefully poured out over a spread of large double sheets of newspaper and then the flowers picked out. Incidentally, it is a good idea to sieve your drying medium from time to time so as to extract any bits of broken material. These may be added to pot-pourri. After brushing away surplus desiccant from the petals, a few light sprays with an aerosol fixative sold for pastel drawings, or an aerosol hair lacquer, is often advantageous, for it brings up the colours, gives a subtle life-like glow to very dry-looking specimens, and imparts additional strength. Hold the spray about a foot away from the subject. When dry, apply a second thin coating all over, front and back and between crevices. Glue back loose petals with a dab of glue.

**Storing material after drying** I find it convenient to store things which have been preserved in desiccant in those rooms in which we live, rather than, for example, guest bedrooms or my flower container room which has no heating. In our main rooms there is free and constant passage of air, sufficient warmth at all times of year, and not very much fear of the arch-enemy of preserved plant material—damp or cold. Garages, sheds, and greenhouses are unsuitable. The airing cupboard is not a good choice of permanent situation as the dryness in the air makes subjects over-brittle and delicate to handle. Flowers in store should be kept away from strong light, as this makes the natural colours fade.

Large cardboard dress boxes or florist's flower boxes make ideal places to store flower heads and tiny stemmed flowers if they can be sub-divided with smaller boxes. As it is vital that the flowers do not crush one another I find it more practical to store stemmed flowers in single layers in large shallow boxes, supported on rolls of tissue paper, rather than piled on top of one another in a deep box. Support bell shapes by stuffing gently with paper tissues. A lid to top the box is important, to keep dust at bay, and flowers stay a good colour in the friendly darkness. A small bag of silica gel granules inside the box will absorb any moisture in the air. It should be replaced and dried off from time to time. Flowers preserved on their own stems or on wired stems may be stored in jugs or similar containers filled with sand or crumpled chicken wire, with a plastic bag right over the top and secured with a rubber band. They can, of course, be arranged straightaway and may be stored inside a large plastic bag until needed; the bag can be inflated by blowing into it, and it is then tied firmly at the neck. Or you can simply put an arrangement out at once to decorate a room. Invariably, desiccant-preserved flower stems get a little curl or a swollen section at the ends. Cut these off to facilitate arranging into foam, etc. Flowers which have been preserved in desiccants should not be arranged with fresh flowers, though a few fresh items may be added to them using florist's tubes etc. for the water.

### Drying in Sand

On the whole, items dried in sand preserve to a good colour, but this method produces a very matt finish. I have found that seaside sand is not really suitable, because of its high salt content, but silver sand (which you can buy from seedsmen) or alternatively fine river sand can be used instead. If you happen to live in a sandy area your local sandpit could be of interest to you. If you buy silver sand it is very fine, and easy to filter down between the flower petals. As it is rather weighty you must take care when pouring it over the flowers; be sure that it supports the petals properly and does not press them down and out of shape. All sand should be very well dried before use by putting it into a very low oven (gas No. $\frac{1}{2}$ or $250°$F. if your cooker is electric) using shallow tins such as clean roasting tins. Depending on the amount of moisture present and the depth of sand in the tin it would take from three to five hours to become bone-dry. Stir it up with a wooden spoon from time to time so that every grain gets a long spell at the top. Electric and coal ovens give best results, having a very dry heat. I have to use gas, which burns with more moisture, and I find my desiccant drying processes take longer. If you can manage it, leaving the sand overnight in a low oven is ideal. Now transfer the slightly cooled sand to deeper tins or plastic boxes, such as biscuit tins, freezer boxes etc.; allow it to cool completely before putting in the plant materials or you will cook them! A good sprinkling of bicarbonate of soda mixed in with the sand helps to fix the petal colour. Lids for the boxes are not required when sand is used.

**Graded grains make finer flowers!** Sand collected economically from the bed of a stream or from a sand-pit must be very fine, as any large granules will pock-mark the petals. If you can get some really fine sand, wash and dry it and then sieve it to remove any large pieces of grit. To wash, fill a deep bowl half-full of sand and add water. Stir well, or swish it around like a gold prospector, to float off dirt and bits of debris. Pour away the water, leaving the sand behind. Repeat several times, then dry very thoroughly. After regular use as a drying medium the sand will need to be dried off again in the oven, to drive off any excess moisture it has absorbed.

### Alum and Borax Mixtures, Salt and Starch

Alum and borax can be bought at the chemist's, and are often recommended for use as desiccants, but there are better methods. They should at any rate always be dried properly before use or they just will not work. Failure with borax alone is often caused by plant material being left in it over-long so that the colour is bleached out, but poor results are generally due to the powder clumping. It should be mixed with sand and/or alum; three parts of sand or alum to one of borax. Alum is sometimes used on its own as a desiccant. If you can buy corn meal, use two parts yellow corn meal to two parts borax with six tablespoonfuls of salt. I find it a good plan to add a little insect killing powder to the drying agent as an insect preventative when using corn meal. Plant material will also dry in salt or powdered starch. All these items must be truly dry at all times. When using these products the lid should be left off the box while preserving takes place.

*Brush desiccant particles from petals after drying.*

Starch tends to stick to petals. Brush it gently away with a small brush, then spray with poster varnish.

## Silica Gel and Named Products

Silica gel is a highly porous material sold in granular and powdered forms. It has a sponge-like quality and great powers of absorption, and extraordinary drying qualities, for it can absorb up to 50 per cent. of its own weight in water and there is no change in size or shape of the particles as, over the months in use, they become saturated. In this, silica gel has distinct advantages over the other drying agents described, which tend to clog together when filled with moisture. It may be reactivated by heating for a period, at a temperature not exceeding 250°F., or No. $\frac{1}{2}$ if you are using gas. The various trade-named products are very similar, and most, I believe, contain silica gel. If sold specially for drying flowers silica gel sometimes comes with a moisture indicator of litmus paper, more usually with bright blue indicator crystals which gradually fade to white and then pink-grey as moisture is absorbed. It is better not to let the desiccant get to the pink-grey stage before putting it into the oven for reactivating.

Use shallow tins for reactivating, rather than very deep ones, and keep turning the desiccant with a wooden spoon. The top indicator crystals soon turn blue, but those underneath remain white. Until all are of a uniform blue again the tins must remain in the oven. In use, flower colours are livelier when the powder is showing a good blue, as drying is then at its speediest. When newly bought or freshly reactivated, the drying action is harsher, and while this is perfect for large, well-built flowers such as roses, dahlias, etc., very small, delicate subjects such as field daisies and forget-me-nots, with their tiny petals, are best preserved in slightly older desiccant where the action is more gentle so that the flowers become less brittle.

Silica gel can be bought from the larger chemists in granular form, for it is sold as a rust preventative for winter storage of lawn mowers. I do not really commend the granular form, for like the coarse-grained sand it tends to pock-mark petals. A friend tried to grind down the granules in the grinding part of her food mixer but the machine got very hot and began to give off a thin ribbon of smoke, and she was put off trying this again! Another friend crushes the grains with a rolling pin, but I do not think this is completely successful as one cannot crush them to a fine enough powder. Another disadvantage is that the tins of granulated silica gel contain only small amounts, so that one is able to preserve only a small number of subjects at a time.

Silica gel is best bought in powder form. When new it smells dry and slightly pungent when disturbed. As I normally kneel on the floor over it when preserving, it used to occur to me to wonder whether it was harmful to breathe it in. However, it seems to have done me no harm, though I have been using it regularly for many years, but obviously one should take care not to inhale it. Being a drying agent it does, of course, ruin your hands, making them very dry. I always try to work in rubber gloves.

**For that special flower** In my opinion, silica gel and the products containing it give the best results of all the drying agents. Those flowers which can be preserved in it have extreme beauty, with every little petal retaining its contours, every stamen erect, usually every subtlety of colour retained, every vein in every leaf, and every tendril intact and completely life-like. The effects are breath-taking. This is a most satisfactory way of preserving a special gift flower, or even a whole bouquet of suitable subjects. In the case of a complete bride's bouquet, simply submerge it in the desiccant as it is. It should be as fresh as possible or you will not be so successful. Generally, however, a bouquet will include white flowers, or some large-faced or intricate flowers such as orchids, which will tend to collapse after a time. On the whole it is best to remove the smaller and more suitable flowers and preserve these, making them up either into a special picture (perhaps a mock bouquet with a frill of lace and tied with bridal ribbons), as a lasting keepsake, or into porcelain flowers as described later. Flower heads are all that are required for making pictures, calendars, and the like. Many people only ever dry flower heads, even for arranging, providing false stems for their larger flowers, either before or after preserving. But in fact the majority of stems can easily be preserved, so

*Every wrinkle in the primrose leaves is retained here after silica gel treatment. The 'tree' preserved itself, as did the moss covering the pinholder. The tiny stile is quickly made from bits of a wooden box held firm on pinholders.*

long as the subjects are kept in the desiccant until the stems as well as the flowers are completely dry to the touch. Not very many flowers have stems which are so thick and juicy as to make preserving them practically impossible, but these include hyacinths, whose flowers, however, dry individually perfectly well. Indeed, hyacinth pips are a particular joy when preserved. Even daffodil stalks will dry, though if you plan to preserve a number they may make it necessary to reactivate your powder fairly frequently. At least you can dry off the thinner top section of the daffodil stem, with its little papery sheath, for these when left intact give any arrangement a great feeling of naturalness.

Thick stems or very juicy leaves such as those of *Begonia rex* will take up to a fortnight, perhaps even longer, to dry off properly, especially if the drying medium is not fresh. Thinner and less squashy subjects preserve more speedily, and if you have a box large enough—and sufficient desiccant—even large sprays of leaves can be tackled.

**Colour retention** Plant materials are positioned in the preserving boxes in exactly the same way as described for using sand and other agents, and then placed in the airing cupboard. When silica gel is being used the boxes must have tight-fitting lids. When removed, flowers will be found to have good colour. Blues generally stay exactly as they were, retaining true colour for many years. I have a fifteen-year-old dried flower picture which includes forget-me-nots, gentians and cornflowers in as lovely hues as the day they were picked in the garden. When a friend and I bought our first silica gel, many years ago, we were enchanted with all that it opened up to us. (It is a good plan, by the way, for two friends to go shares with a large tin.) We would telephone each other daily to report on our latest successes. 'Have you tried wild roses yet?' I would ask excitedly. 'No, but polyanthus are extremely good,' she would reply, 'though the red ones tend to turn rather dark.' We had much fun experimenting with everything which came to hand, and comparing notes.

Over the years I have found that colours tend to vary. Some pigments are retained better than others, but most subjects do keep their colour well in silica gel, and the colour usually lasts many months before fading to a variety of creams, browns, dark lavender, palest blue, and soft red, which are not unattractive. Yellows, oranges, pinks, most reds and lavenders preserve well, white is good at first.

## Preserving with Detergents

Ordinary detergent powders can be useful for drying flowers and leaves, and one cup of borax may be added to a large packet. Detergents containing enzymes are perhaps quicker in their drying action, resulting in good colour retention. One called Bold, which can be bought on both sides of the Atlantic, is the one I have used. You need not put the lid on the preserving box during processing.

## Points Worth Remembering

If you own a freezer you will know that when it is a new toy you tend to freeze everything in sight, getting a sort of squirrel-like attitude to food. Watch out for the same thing happening when you first begin preserving flowers in desiccants. Although it is good to experiment, don't do as I did and preserve in such quantity that storage becomes a problem. Far better to preserve small samples of individual items, just to see their capabilities. With larger flowers, preserve a batch sufficient for one arrangement not ten! When storing many small flowers in boxes it helps if you grade similar colours together for see-at-a-glance ease of use. This also protects the tiniest items from damage as searching fingers dig about among larger items.

With some drying mediums there will be a slight alteration in some petal colours. Colour-fastness over a period of time depends to an extent on how the flowers are managed. Those stored in boxes keep good colour, possibly for years; those arranged in a sunny room will fade more rapidly than others standing in a darker corner. When you come to think of it, many items fade in bright light and sunshine, from fabrics to the hairs on our heads. Remember this when positioning dried flowers. Dried flowers under glass will keep a better colour than those open to the air, and those in constant warmth do better than those in conditions of fluctuating warmth. Surprisingly, the colour of most annual plants lasts splendidly; such things as godetia, larkspur, cornflowers, and forget-me-nots being specially worthy in this respect. Reds generally preserve and keep well, particularly orange-reds. Blue-pinks are good. Yellow is excellent, though it can fade with time. Very deep violets and purples may darken considerably while undergoing the process of preservation, but lavender colour is usually good. All orange colours are splendid. Green is satisfactory at first but often softens to grey-green. Grey in time may turn to a pretty yellow-grey or off-white. White is a most disappointing colour, tending to turn to cream or buff quite soon after preserving, although spraying with clear lacquer or varnish helps considerably.

Among flowers and leaves I particularly recommend for preserving are roses, carnations, pinks, red cyclamen, violets, mimosa, anemones (especially the early shop ones), buttercups, and auriculas. Small button chrysanthemums are worth remembering, as

*Interlaced montbretia foliage gives lift and life to old-fashioned pinks in this early summer arrangement. Spraying twice with matt pastel fixative helps strengthen the colouring of the pinks.*

are clematis (particularly the small species ones), crocus, sprays of spring blossom, the white flowers of *Cornus canadensis* (each set off by a little black central boss), flower sprays of montbretia, daphne, delphinium, and trails of hops, flowers of honesty (lunaria), Queen Anne's lace (lovely for adding to bridal pictures), hellebores, ranunculus, Michaelmas daisy, hydrangea, and salvia. Moss and every sort of small fern, as well as the leaves from innumerable house plants, will be found invaluable additions to decorations.

**Material which is difficult** The exact 3-D shape of flowers, leaves, and seedheads is retained when preserved in a desiccant, except for those subjects which have deep bells, such as campanula, deep trumpets such as daffodils, and various lilies, or very loose, large, or open petals such as passion flower, orchids, clematis, and hellebores. Though their shapes may be perfectly retained for many months, especially if atmospheric conditions are right, in the normal way expect them to reabsorb moisture from the air, perhaps on a damp summer's day when there is no central heating in use. Then their tendency is to collapse slightly in upon themselves and they lose their pristine appearance. They are still very well worth preserving, however, even for short periods, but you can help them in various ways to stand up for themselves for much longer spans of time. With some flowers you will find that you can drip melted candle wax, colourless of course, into their centres and over their backs after preserving, or you may neatly wire up the backs of petals, running glue over the wire and then transparent tape. But obviously this is only possible with flowers which have a certain built-in sturdiness and thickness of petal. Some, such as tulips and crocus, can be gently glued so that the petals support each other, then they are sprayed or brushed over lightly with matt poster varnish. Indeed, matt poster varnish, pastel fixative, and hair lacquer can greatly lengthen the life span of most flowers preserved in desiccants. The healthy, life-like, slight luminosity some of these give to the flowers is specially recommended for those flowers which have had a natural gloss in life or ones which, after preservation, appear too matt and dried looking. The slight glow also brings up the full colour of the treated flowers and leaves. It is worth experimenting a little to find out what you feel is acceptable.

### Carrying Flowers to a Show

Carrying flowers which have been preserved in desiccants to a show, is a strange experience. They 'shush' at you as you drive over every rut in the road! It is, on the whole, best to transport such material to a show or other event in boxes, arranging it when you arrive. Otherwise you can place a mass design so that it lies face up on a build-up of pillows, blankets, or garden cushions, or upright in a box with the front cut away and braced by bricks, plastic bags filled with sand, or whatever device your fancy can dream up to support the fragile burden.

## Flowers with the Look of China

To create unusual fine bone china flower effects is not only simple but also preserves the flowers in full beauty of colour and form for very lengthy periods. Such flowers may be confidently arranged in conditions with more humidity than is advisable in the normal way. The colour in these 'china' flowers is emphasised, like the colour of a stone or shell seen through water. To give any preserved flower this glossy porcelain appearance, just spray it all over with three to four coats of clear polyurethane, or picture varnish, holding the aerosol quite close to the flowers. Leave to dry out between each spraying. It may be necessary to re-spray with the varnish from time to time as the original loses its first lustre. The effect is particularly delightful in any flower which has patterning, such as spotting or veining on a ground colour. Leaves are not perhaps so effective, looking a little like cheap plastic. In any case, the contrast between dull-surfaced leaves and softly glossy flowers is attractive. An arrangement of 'china' flowers is effective in a china container, and might be a good way of interpreting one of those favourite classes in flower shows, 'An arrangement to complement a piece of china'. You should, of course, try to use similar flowers to those on the piece of china itself. Fresh flowers may be glossed similarly, but the effect is more glass like and less spectacular, although some fresh leaves such as ivy and other evergreens and sturdy-textured foliage from pot plants, can be very pleasing, and the varnish acts as an instant preservative.

## Making Flower Pictures

Flowers preserved in desiccants are ideal for making into pictures and calendars. As the plant forms are completely three dimensional, if glass is to be used over them some clearance is necessary so that the flowers are not touched or squashed. Frames with bevelled glass are ideal, as are box-like frames with a slight depth to them. Husbands or handymen can sometimes produce the latter for you and they can be bought. As flowers dried in desiccants keep their colour very true and for a lengthy time, after they have lost their first brittleness they may be pressed between newspaper under heavy books or bricks and used as described under pressed flowers.

When local flower arrangers put on a preserved flower festival in a small manor house not only did their work include everything from large elegant pedestals down to miniature delights in thimbles and such, they also decorated brooches, lampshades, mirrors, and gift boxes with desiccant-dried plant forms. And anyone, anywhere, can follow suit!

# By Special Arrangement

**Method 9** *Drying in Arrangement and in Hot Spots*

Maybe all of us have, at one time or another, been lax and allowed a fresh flower arrangement to dry out, forgetting to top up the water level as we should, and have been surprised to find that on discarding it one or two items have miraculously preserved themselves. I find that in late summer and autumn, during very dry spells, when the growth of plant life slows down and petals thicken and assume a firmer texture and colour, even small roses and button chrysanthemums, zinnias, smaller double dahlias, heather, and flowers with close-packed petals and firm stems, will sometimes do this if I deliberately allow the water to evaporate.

Conditions indoors must be extra warm for a good rate of success, and stems should preferably be of a tough, and better still woody, nature rather than squashy. Petals must be taken by surprise and dried before they have time to contemplate wilting! Arrange in shallow water or wet flower-arranging foam, in a container, which is then placed very close, perhaps immediately above, some source of heat, such as a central heating radiator. In this manner some flowers and seedheads will preserve themselves quite quickly. A way with other flowers is to press short stems on to the pins of a pinholder, which is then put directly on top of the warm tank or a radiator, out of water.

The chenille-like seedheads of sumach (cotinus), and love-lies-bleeding (amaranthus) dry very easily in arrangements, and make good forms for future designs, the plush sumach standing erect, often on gaily twisting stems, in a completely life-like manner. The love-lies-bleeding drips in interesting waterfall effects. Divide very heavily flowered stems into shorter sections before drying. Both it and sumach will also dry easily by hanging (Method 7). Try, also, sprays of fuchsia, some ranunculus (particularly red ones), achillea, small-flowered clematis, cyclamen, delphinium, and the leaf rosettes of London pride (*Saxifraga umbrosa*), and leaf rosettes and heads of verbascum and *Stachys lanata*.

**Dry them up to Christmas** Another way is to put suitable subjects directly on to a night storage radiator or similar hot spot with crumpled tissue paper under the flower heads to prevent scorching of delicate petals. Some flowers will shrink a little, and so will stems. All will preserve within a day or two, generally keeping good shape and excellent natural colour, although white flowers are not recommended. Red flowers and blue ones are perhaps the most successful I've tried. Small red roses and double red ranunculus

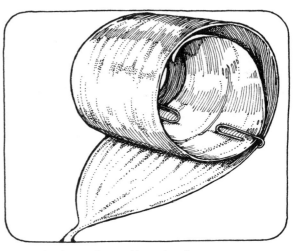

*Leaves dried in curls provide variety for arrangement.*

*Enjoy a design of preserving leaves at summer's close. Here fresh water iris leaves and hosta are arranged in water which is slowly allowed to dry away. Note the wedge of leaf at the front—a good way to support a wayward stem!*

are special favourites of mine, and I have dried garden roses this way right up to Christmas Day to provide a posy for my desk or a little table. One must experiment, but I think you will be surprised at the flowers it is possible to preserve in these ways. Naturally you will use discretion, not putting the drying subjects over the grille of a heater, and drying out only a small quantity at a time, so that a close eye can be kept on the process. Fire risks would deter me if I had small children likely to tamper with the process or if the radiator stood close to a draughty door, but something can usually be arranged. The unlagged tank in the airing cupboard is particularly satisfactory, except that its top is generally rounded.

Among foliage which will preserve well this way is aspidistra cut fresh from a pot plant, iris, broom, pinned curls of *Phormium tenax*, and both curly kale and lily-of-the-valley dry to a very good green. Some of this foliage can be coaxed into curves, curls and spirals before drying. Hold the curl shapes during the drying process with paper clips. For extra interest, some arrangers like to cut or slit their larger preserved leaves, creating new patterns from the basic shapes, but this is obviously something about which you can decide for yourself.

**Drying eucalyptus in arrangement** Some foliage will dry out successfully in an arrangement, becoming almost indestructible. Ficus leaves, for example, taken from the base of a pot plant, will dry beautifully in water or out of it, changing slowly from green to delicate tans and creams. *Eucalyptus gunnii* is popularly grown by many arrangers. They either cut the growing tree back regularly, so that it becomes a thick shrub with round blue-grey juvenile leaves, or they allow it to run up to tree size, when the shape of the leaves alters, becoming more sickle shaped. The stems turn silvery blue and flowers are followed by amusing little seedheads. Cut at any stage, arrange it in a little water, and allow it to dry off. Only the very tiniest baby leaves at the top of the sprays will collapse on you. The delicate colour is well preserved and proves invaluable for many flower-pieces. It can also be bought fresh from time to time at any good florist's, but a friend with a mature specimen in her garden will always be happy to cut you a spray or two. Eucalyptus will also preserve well by Method 2 (glycerine) but the colour is altered, though there is the advantage that the sprays remain pliable.

Among many other evergreens with the same good-natured habit of preserving themselves in an arrangement in a little water are all the conifers. Though after a time the colour may soften a trifle, this often does not matter. At Christmas a delicate 'frosting', a puff of gold or silver, matt oxblood, blue-green and bronze, or what you will from an aerosol spray or poster paint gives fresh spirit to such leaves. I find that foliage so coloured is even lovelier in following years, if I can store it carefully, for the colour quietens and becomes more subtle as time passes. *Hebe armstrongii*, with its olive-yellow whipcord foliage, and *Hebe hectori*, which is similar in colour and form, preserve nicely in a little water, as they will in glycerine (Method 2) or in one of the desiccants (Method 8). Branches of pine will also dry off while in an arrangement and a light spray over with a fixative for charcoal drawings, which can be obtained from an art shop, puts back a healthy glow and strengthens the colour.

**Preserving hosta leaves** Hosta leaves undulate and curl, making fantastic fan and twisted cape-like shapes as they dry out slowly in an arrangement with water. Though they will be rather brittle, with care you will find them invaluable for providing strength of shape, strong character, and swirling movement to late summer designs of zinnias, chrysanthemums, roses, etc. The ribs are specially handsome, and those leaves which curl inwards like tiny cigars provide yet new shapes to these familiar leaves. The Ikebana arrangers sometimes curl fresh hosta leaves, rolling them round a slim pencil, and I have sometimes coaxed one or two leaves to take on this controlled shape in the following way. Hold the shape with a paper clip until the leaf is quite dried out. The leaf colour changes from the original green to cream or a soft yellow and finally to a delicate tan. The results all along the way are good, an arrangement of the preserving leaves altering weekly and giving much pleasure.

The cast iron plant (aspidistra) is another trouble-free leaf which can be arranged in water to dry out slowly, losing the green colour eventually and turning a pleasing tan. Palms can be dried in arrangement, in a little water. Big fan palm leaves can be cut down to make two or three from one. They last for ever after drying.

Leafless sprays of *Rosa omeiensis pteracantha*, with its huge scarlet thorns, dry splendidly, or can be glycerined. Croton, too, will dry off in a little water. Mare's tail dries nicely in arrangement. Don't throw discarded pieces on to your garden rubbish heap or you will get a colony of this pest springing up.

The stems of some dogwood (cornus) take on attractive colourings in winter; their cheerful stems are whippy and easily curved into swirling light-hearted loops, ribbons, and S-bends, to dry off in these shapes in an arrangement.

**Globe artichokes and cardoons** Globe artichoke (*Cynara scolymus*) and cardoon (*Cynara cardunculus*) make splendid 'wooden flowers' and buds. They are very alike and provide violet-blue flowers like great

thistles, then going on to become honey-coloured seedheads of six inches or so across, all of which can be preserved. I buy globe artichokes in the green bud stage from the supermarket, coax the leathery green 'petals' apart, putting small wads of newspaper between them, to preserve the flower-like effect. I leave some semi-padded like half-open flowers, and dry others as pointed buds. Placed directly on a radiator or airing tank, they look very handsome and intriguing in the process of preservation. This takes some weeks owing to their thickness. The newspaper is slowly removed as the heads dry. The green changes to a rich wood colour and, once preserved, the material seems to last for ever. It may be gilded, or dyed by soaking in hot water dye.

To preserve the purple-blue flower heads, gather them from the garden just as the petals push from the scaly buds and shortly after. If left over-long, the blue when preserved tends to a greyer appearance, and the heads may go to seed. To preserve the big powder-puff seedheads, again gather early and dry as quickly as possible by hanging over direct heat (Method 7), or they disperse into a hundred dandelion-like 'clocks'. This can to some extent be prevented by a light spraying with hair lacquer or charcoal fixative. An even better method of preservation is in glycerine. If left in the garden to 'go over' there is still something of interest; gently remove the jaded fluff and old central portions from the head, to win for yourself a flower-like item on a long stem, lovely to dry off for a large flower group. I have said rather a lot about cynara, but they do have quite a lot going for them in my affections.

**Delphinium and larkspur** Spires of delphinium and larkspur in flower will dry off speedily in water immediately over a source of heat, though they are more usually dried by hanging (Method 7), I have found my method is just as successful. Any petals which crease may be very gently smoothed out. Individual delphinium florets may be dried in the same way, out of water, face down on crumpled tissue, or better still in a drying agent (Method 8). Catananche, or Cupid's dart, is another good subject. Often left to dry on the plant, in fact the shuttlecocks of blue or white preserve far better in shallow water in an arrangement. If picked too early they may not attain full colour, too late and the colour dries to dingy grey.

**Hydrangeas like summer seas** Hydrangea flower heads can be dried in a number of ways, the colour lasting for a long time particularly if not exposed to sunlight. Pick in late summer when the petals (really long-lasting sepals) have more 'body', feeling slightly leathery and firmer to the touch than they do when younger. Once you get the feel you will recognise it again another year. Test the bushes each week, cupping maturing heads in your hands until one day your fingers curl round petals which feel not quite so alive and fresh as they did last time. I would leave them another week just to be on the safe side if this is your first time. There is no hurry; the natural maturing process lasts for some weeks, and flowers can be preserved during this time. Better to err on the side of maturity than immaturity, for blooms which are not quite ready will never preserve by this method.

As the stalks will dry, cut the heads on varying stem lengths. You can leave on one or two leaves, for these will often preserve reasonably well. It will be found helpful to select a variety of sizes in the flower heads if possible. Too many large moppity ones are really quite difficult to accommodate in arrangements for today's smaller rooms. Or you can break down the large heads into smaller components, if you wish. If you require only individual flowers, for calendars and so on, snip off pieces of heads. When gathering from your shrubs, resist the merry urge to cut every flower on a long stalk. The buds for next year's flowers are high on the stems, not far beneath the current heads— it is as well to leave some behind for next year's harvest.

After cutting, I put my flower heads in a jug with a little water and stand this in the airing cupboard for a few days. When the bun-shaped heads feel crackling dry to the touch they can be removed and gently laid on crumpled tissues, on a shelf in the airing cupboard, as the juicy stems take a little longer to dry off completely. In my own airing cupboard there is a slit between two of the boards making up one shelf, and I slip the stems through this so that they dangle free in the warm air, the already preserved heads being supported by the shelf itself. Another way is to push the preserved heads through a length of plastic-covered chicken wire or even a cake-cooling tray, suspended from hooks in the airing cupboard.

It is generally the mop-headed florist's hydrangea (*Hydrangea macrophylla*) which people preserve this way, but other kinds do equally well. All flowers left on the shrubs turn brown in early winter, but pieces may still be gathered, dried off for a day or two in the airing cupboard out of water, and then given new life styles by spraying with soft metallic blue-green or cream and pink paints. At a flower festival early last summer a friend had made up a patriotically-coloured pedestal arrangement with gorgeous clear blue hydrangea, white roses, and red geraniums. She had cleverly achieved her blue hydrangea colour with the help of a well-directed spray of matt car-body paint. It is usually the light, gay, blue, which reminds one of summer seas that most flower arrangers find desirable, and as this blue comes only when hydrangeas are grown in non-alkaline soils, or when watered with doses of colourant, I think it is quite a good plan to spray-paint the dried heads when the occasion demands. The creamy-green, sea-blue, and baby-ribbon pink of a very young hydrangea head is most appealing, and can be perfectly retained by Method 8 (with a desiccant).

## Preserving Fruit–Gourds

A number of different fruits can be preserved in the warmth of airing cupboard or radiator. Gourds are most popularly grown by flower arrangers for winter colour, but people are sometimes nervous as to how to harvest them correctly. Every year I receive hundreds of letters on this. Handle gourds at all stages as if they were made of the most delicate china, for they will bruise and rot internally after suffering any rough handling. Pick them when fully ripe, or again they are liable to rot. I generally leave mine on the vines until autumn, picking them just before first frosts, though light frost does not seem to cause much harm. Incidentally, I have successfully altered the shape of growing gourds by taping the long ones into curves with freezer tape. If picked with a section of stem left on, these will usually preserve with a curve, giving the gourd a slightly saucy look which can be appealing. Gourds can be varnished with a spray of clear varnish or polyurethane, or even hair lacquer. The sprays are specially useful for warty gourds! But the glossy effect is not pleasing to everyone and it is debatable as to whether it gives longer life; it certainly does not prevent decay in a bruised gourd. Spray with pastel fixative for matt effects. Anyway, arranged on a wicker tray, in a copper pan, or a wooden bowl, they make a glowing decoration, looking equally at home in a country house or a town flat. They last colourfully for a very long time and slowly dry off in such an arrangement. Do not puncture the skins. The advice to wire gourds with a false stem at their newly picked stage is wrong, for they will rot off at the point of puncture.

When absolutely dry they feel light as air and lose most or all of their rich colour, changing to gentle buffs, quiet greens and browns, and faded golds; their seeds rattle away inside and at this stage they can certainly be wired. Painted, they make amusing Christmas tree decorations, but are still handsome if gently rubbed over with brown stain shoe polish to give depth to the colour. I rub this up with a soft shoe brush to get a warm glow, repeating this until I achieve the colour I like. Dried gourds may also be bleached (page 31) or coloured with shoe dyes. Lovely added to swags and preserved designs, they are ideal for abstract as well as traditional work. Being light in weight when completely dry, they are excellent for swinging mobiles and for wall collages, when they are exceptionally interesting cut in half to show the seeds.

**Squashes and luffas** Squashes take even longer to dry off properly. I was once given a large one which remained heavy and true to colour–like a great

*Gourds are available in many shapes and patterns.*

*Grow a few cucumber-like plants of luffa, the vegetable sponge, in the greenhouse or, easier still, buy its seed cases at the chemist! Here the left-hand pieces have been soaked and bent to new shapes, after cutting them open to expose the interesting internal structures. Dried seaweed stems and glass pieces are assembled together on a flat shell to suggest an underwater world of strange forms and textures. The colour of dried luffas can be altered with car-body paints.*

golden moon–for over five years. Actually I lost it in the end when I dropped it while bringing it home from St Paul's Cathedral, where it had played a part in a flower festival. It immediately began to rot, but I dried the remains in the airing cupboard. If, after picking gourds, squashes, etc., they do begin to become mildewed, all is not lost; only the colour need be sacrificed if you rub away the mould and leave the fruits for a couple of weeks on top of your hot spot. This will stop the decay, unless it is very far advanced, and the fruit when dry will be usable; any discoloura-tion can be quite effective when used dramatically in an arrangement. Dried gourds and squashes which get partially broken open, exposing their seeds, can make forceful additions to designs of an interpretative nature in spring and autumn.

A useful container may be created from a large squash by scraping out the inside, drying the shell, then lacquering or varnishing it. Here is a little list of gourds you might like to consider growing. They are grown each year from seed and make rambling plants for a sunny trellis or fence. If grown on the ground they tend to get terribly dirty and eaten by passing slugs. Turban and Chinese gourds are large fellows of orange, red, and yellow, like turbans in shape and colour. The club gourds and mixed pear-shaped describe themselves. There are warted gourds, sometimes with green and yellow stripes on white, syphon or dipper gourds, and spoon gourds too. Buy the seeds in packets of distinct types or a mixed packet containing a variety.

Luffas bought from chemist's shops make ideal material for modern designs. (After soaking flat ones in water to plump them up, dry again.) They are the skeletons of cucumber-like plants and are natural plant material. You can grow them from seed in a green-house in cold climates. They must be ripe before gathering or will lack rigidity. Remove peel and wash away pulp. Dry and spray-paint them for modern decorations, and cut them into new shapes. They may be soaked in water and re-shaped to make new forms, suggesting sea corals. The fruiting heads or cobs of sweet corn and other decorative corns can be dried slowly in arrangement or by hanging (Method 7). These are such an asset to your dried flower boxes and

44

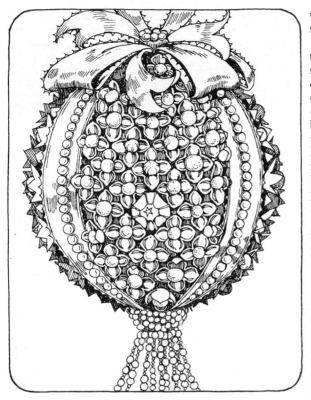

*Pomanders are easily made from cloves and oranges.*

are great fun to have. Indian or squaw corn is quite unbelievable, with its multi-coloured kernels of slate blue, mahogany, brown, red and gold. These fantastic things are nicely set off by the outer sheaths, which dry to the colour of cream. I pull the sheath gently back from the cob, cutting it down to suitable size, like petals. I deal similarly with strawberry corn, a corn shaped like a very big luscious loganberry, with hairs!

**A garland of lemons** Among fruits which will easily preserve on a shelf in the airing cupboard or on a radiator are capsicum, pineapple tops and lemons. Soft-skinned fruits must not be put directly on a hot surface, but should be protected with crumpled tissue. I once had to make an arrangement to include preserved lemons because it was to stand in a cathedral near a Della Robbia plaque garlanded with pottery lemons. I found that the fruits dried naturally arranged on a tray in my kitchen and retained their shapes although they shrank a little, and the colouring became darker. A little help from tubes of green and yellow oil paint rubbed well in solved the colour problem. But I think my favourite fruits for preserving are pomegranates; I add to my collection every year, buying the fruits from the greengrocer's and drying them in my hot spots. They retain their form and texture excellently, and their colour is good for years. Choose

unblemished, unbruised fruits, of course. Those with softly blushing skins are prettiest.

Fruits of ivy, fruiting stems of Solomon's seal (with the foliage removed), winged seed sprays of maple and sycamore, the tiny purple bead-like berries of callicarpa, all preserve with ease in an arrangement with or without water. *Iris foetidissima* seedheads split open dramatically when ripe, to expose the show-off orange berries against a cream inside. They are very lovely, but tend to drop fairly quickly if left on the plants overlong or handled too much. Arrange them normally in a little water after gently varnishing over the berries with colourless nail varnish, or spraying with picture varnish. It is difficult to preserve most berries in anything but glycerine (Method 2), which alters their colour, and they tend to shrink if a drying agent is used. I find the best way is to spray them with clear polyurethane or hair lacquer, or paint them with colourless nail varnish, which keeps them beautiful for many months.

**Making pomanders** In Britain for centuries oranges have been preserved by sticking them all over with rows of cloves to make deliciously fragrant mothpreventatives. In earlier times they were carried about in the hand to mask the smells of open drains and protect against the plague and other infections. A bowl full of pomanders makes a delightful decoration for the house and a boxed pomander is an acceptable Christmas or birthday present. I often make an elegant jewelled one with pearls and broken beads stuck among the cloves and with a bright ribbon so that it can be hung up in a winter window. I also make a number decorated with jewels or gaily coloured dried flowers as a smart decoration for a grown-ups' Christmas tree. Impaled on curved stems made from cane, they become fascinating new forms for arrangers to use in arrangements. Pomanders sell very readily at bazaars and make unusual items for including in dried harvest decorations. Generally acceptable as plant material in competition work in Britain (cloves are the commercially dried buds of a flowering tree and are therefore plant material), pomanders are easily made. Simply stick the cloves all over a large, thin-skinned orange and dry in a hot spot. To make a ribbon hanging, square off the orange with ribbon, knotting the ribbon at the top and pinning it into place with straight pins or short pieces of florist's wire. Cloves act as a preservative, and even the bits underneath the ribbon will not 'go off'. My godmother preserved oranges this way all her life, and when she died I found some in her wardrobe which must have been over 40 years old. I still have them in my own wardrobe, keeping moths at bay.

After writing an article on the subject for a gardening journal I was besieged with letters, including one from a reader who told me that years ago her family made apple pomanders in the same way, studding hard, good-keeping varieties with cloves, tying them with red ribbons, and giving them as gifts to Hallowe'en and Christmas party guests. Lemons can be preserved similarly and look lovely arranged together in a pottery dish of an earthy colour.

## Preserving Decorative Fungi

Fungi are strange and eye-catching. When found fresh and in good condition, before they have become over-ripe or drilled into by beetles and things, they will dry. Many become rock-hard and will remain shapely for years. They may be used for covering the mechanics in an arrangement or as design elements in their own right. It is vital to dry them very quickly on radiators or in the airing cupboard; this not only preserves the fungi but kills off any boring insects which might be lurking in them. The process should take two to three weeks, and the scent of some as they dry is perfectly frightful! For this reason I often seal them first in plastic bags and hang them in the airing cupboard immediately above the warm tank. *Polystictus versicolor* (sorry about the name) being of a cork-like nature dries within a week, while *Polyporus betulinus*, mostly found on old birch tree trunks, may take up to three weeks; by the way, this last used to be dried for stropping razors. I think it wise to check with a book on fungi before tampering with the unknown. Some fungi are poisonous and however colourful and amusing they may be in shape, even when dry the poisonous properties may be retained. Edible mushrooms and small wild fungi dry well in silica gel (Method 8).

## Dried Seaweed Roots and Plumes

Dried seaweed roots and plumes can be useful in some designs. They may be re-shaped after soaking in warm water, then allowed to dry. Obviously they must not be arranged in water again unless provided with artificial stems to hold them clear of the water. Interesting curves and twists can be made by winding soaked seaweed around a slim container or jar and allowing it to dry *in situ*.

Plants which happily dry out more or less naturally indoors to pleasant colours and shapes have been welcomed for home and church decoration for centuries. The winter vogue for a sheaf of brown bulrushes (cat's-tail, typha) arranged spikily in a tall trumpet-shaped vase appeared in Victorian times and proved very popular, though bulrushes were used as decoration long before this. They are still popular with today's arrangers, for they make useful slender 'tops' of arrangements such as pedestals in autumn and winter, being equally attractive in shallow dishes arranged, perhaps, with just a few flowers or leaves in naturalistic style. Gather them in good time, although you may find if you pick the smaller ones too early that the whole head shrinks while drying, in the end providing little but a funny stick with one end slightly thickened! If left over-long on the plant all of them will fluff, showering fine seeds round a room. Some years ago I ran the sales table at my flower arrangement club. One day we were given a great sheaf of slightly suspect bulrushes–suspect because of a small tell-tale looseness in the brown plush tops. A member who bought them, took them home on a fairly long journey in a country bus. To her everlasting amusement but temporary embarrassment, the winter warmth of the bus brought her over-ripe bulrushes to fulfilment, and they shed hundreds of fluffy seeds throughout the lower deck. A nice story to help you remember to leave well alone if you get the chance of a bouquet of over-ripe bulrushes. An easy test is to rub your finger up and down the plush. If there is the slightest indication of 'give' a spray with hair lacquer or charcoal fixative will hold things temporarily, but the resulting mess should the fluff begin to fly is just not worth the effort involved. Gathered at the correct time, when the heads are fat and perfect, they will preserve either in an arrangement with or without a little water in a cool place, by hanging upside down (Method 7) or in glycerine (Method 2). Then they are superb. Cut in May for a yellow-green colour, in June for tan, and early autumn for rich brown.

## Preserving Lichens and Mosses

A treasure from heath and moorland is blue-grey reindeer or Iceland moss, which can also be bought dried at the florist's. When bought it must first be damped down to bring out its best colour and allow it to expand. Stand it on the lawn during a spell of damp weather, or leave it soaking in a bowl of water and then drain and dry it once more on a cake-cooling tray. Thick, hoary-looking lichen found on the black stems of old apple and thorn trees in some country areas is equally desirable. Brought indoors, it will dry quickly in an arrangement. I went to a friend's home the other day and admired frilly lichened branches arranged like a tree, under which preserved pink roses blossomed. Two artificial birds with pink breasts completed the picture. Such a design would last the winter, the flowers being changed from time to time to avoid monotony. If lichen fades after a few years, spray it lightly with blue/metallic-green paint. As when painting any plant form, however, try not to let your enthusiasm carry you away. The effect is generally best, except sometimes for ultra-modern work, when you underplay rather than overplay on colour.

Cool mosses found on old tree stumps and walls

*Field grasses (dried by Method 3), corn, berries, a bergenia leaf, sweet corn and two pomanders on a flat, hand-made basket base, link up well in colour and texture with the Italian raffia cockerel.*

can be dried by easing off sizeable portions and leaving in a quick-dry place for a few days. The quicker you dry, the better will the colour be retained. Mosses growing on earth are not quite so usable, as they tend to drop dry soil everywhere. Mossy stones and lichened tree barks make ideal cover-ups for mechanics in many a dried group. Moss with fruiting portions is specially interesting for the making of dried flower pictures, when preserved individually as an additional tiny detail.

**Pampas Grass and Cereals**

Grasses of all kinds, including pampas (cortaderia), sea lyme grass (elymus), the small cream plumes of gardener's garters (*Phalaris arundinacea picta*), cereals, such as oats, wheat, and barley, may be picked and arranged indoors out of water for you to enjoy as they go about the business of preserving themselves. They may also be dried by hanging or pressing. I prefer to pick grasses as they escape from their protective sheaths of green or cream. This way, they open sufficiently in the warmth of the house and do not discard bits all over the carpets. Pampas grass can be a luxurious alive-looking silky-silver thing, or a dull plume, like lank and dirty hair. Pick it just as it is about to unfurl, or when half unfurled, no later, and you will see it at its most lovely. It makes a good bold lead-in shape for the top of a pedestal arrangement or other large design, and is a lovely thing with light flowing through it from behind. It is one of the few items I know which looks well at night in a window, seen against the darkness outside. If the plumes are pulled into pieces they create airy flyaway outline effects for small designs. Even the tiniest wisps can find their way into calendars and so on. Pampas, though attractive when allowed to dry itself out in a waterless container, preserves even better in glycerine (Method 2), as perhaps do the majority of grasses, for this keeps them silky soft and they do not drop.

Unless you wish to make hay while the sun shines, do not dry grasses in full sunlight. Select only well-shaped good-sized grass heads for preserving. Too many indeterminate varieties, with small fussy heads, add very little to the majority of flower decorations. Such things as cloud grass (*Agrostis nebulosa*) though attractive enough in itself is really too fine for practical use, being lost among its neighbours when arranged. The cut stalks of many wild field grasses are ever-useful for making into stems for mock posies and bouquets in framed pictures etc. Hollow sections of stem make false stalks for flowers and leaves preserved without their own stems, or for extending shorter ones. A jar of such stalks should be near to everyone's boxes of preserved flowers.

A wide variety of grasses may be grown from seed. Among them I can specially commend pennisetum, with white and purplish feather-duster plumes;

setaria, with foxy-gold sprays which, heavy with seed, present a cascade effect; briza, the quaking grass; panicum, which is green and violet and reminds me of a school play in which I once took part–I was an Egyptian with a flail! *Tricholaena rosea*, which has silky wine-coloured spikes; lagurus, the hare's tail grass, always popular; koeleria, the blue meadow grass, which has quite bright blue-green panicles which will later turn to an attractive brown; *Zea mays japonica*, similar to maize when in flower and which, like its ribbon-resembling foliage, preserves well (the latter particularly noteworthy when preserved in glycerine). A pack of mixed seed gives some variety. Other good grasses for our purpose include perennial *Miscanthus zebrinus*, which has airy heads on long stems; *Elymus glaucus*, a graceful grass with blue-grey flowers, excellent for drying; and *Stipa gigantea*, with heads of 'golden oats'. Grasses which tend to drop when dried may be gently sprayed with hair lacquer, or pastel fixatives, but if picked at the correct time and preserved properly they should not suffer this fault.

**Dyeing grasses** Every year I receive a host of letters asking how to dye grasses. I find that some do not take colour very easily, and it is a good plan to observe the types which are successfully coloured commercially. Some grasses are unsuitable because they absorb the colourant, gaining a dull and cheerless effect. Cut them, dry them, then spray with an aerosol car paint–reds, oranges, and blues are particularly successful. For more delicate colours, leave the dried grasses soaking in detergent water for about an hour, then drain. Now submerge them in a small bath or bowl of hot water alkaline dye until the desired strength of colour is attained. This will only be a short time for very soft colours. Leave them to dry thoroughly on a cake-cooling tray.

And so I come to the end of my section of this book. You are now on your own to dabble about and enjoy yourself in your own way! I am absolutely sure that you will find this particular facet of flower arranging an exciting, intriguing and truly inspiring one, with still many discoveries to be made. I send you my very best wishes and I hope that every flower you preserve is as lovely as the moment when you picked it–for that, I'm sure you'll agree, is the simple yardstick against which we must always measure our success.

*The large variety of shapes and sizes of grasses and seedheads make them exciting and easy subjects for drying, with many uses in all kinds of arrangement.*

# Pressing Flowers

*I would keep these lovely flowers*
*Their beauty to behold,*
*Beyond their sweet short natural hour*
*Time touches some with gold.*

RENEE BURGESS

# The Fascination of Pressing Flowers

Flowers and leaves are so wonderfully and intricately formed that efforts have been made to capture and preserve their beauty for something like two centuries, even before Victorian ladies made 'phantom bouquets', which just occasionally can be found in the antique shops. These little pictures were of skeletonised leaves on black velvet with a few flowers tucked in the centre and tied with a ribbon bow.

Posies still make charming pressed-flower pictures but owing to the great interest in flower arranging we have become more conscious of the various shapes in nature and the possibilities offered in the way of arranging them, so that we are now more adventurous and try to use the flowers and foliage not only as a florist might, but also in the manner of an artist. No doubt in time – when these pictures themselves are dated – a way will be found to press and preserve all the living colour of plants, possibly by the use of transparent resins, but perversely I find the all-over mellowed shades, which can make an old picture look something like inlay or marquetry, very pleasing.

If you love flowers – and I think you must if you are reading this book – then the making of pictures with pressed plant material will give you a great deal of pleasure. You will discover the fascinating detail of each flower, learning to know flowers much more intimately even though you already use them often in arrangements at home. This is because as well as pressing, for example, complete rounded daisy-shaped flowers, it is necessary to take others to pieces, sometimes because the centre would be too bulky to press, and also because the individual shape and beauty of the petals can be lost if not pressed singly. These can be re-assembled to make a shape like the original flower, or made up in quite a different flower shape. Not that I am suggesting that one can improve on Nature – but just to cheat a little, and use the material so that it shows to best advantage.

Petals only slightly overlapping can make a very pleasing pattern, whereas a double layer, or more, can look muddled. I'm sure you will be enchanted with the detail of flowers such as astrantia (it really is a miniature work of art) the silky bracts of *Anemone pulsatilla* and the delicate veining of petals as found in the pelargonium variety Carisbrooke, especially when you open the pressing papers to find that two single petals have moved together as you disturbed them and at once they suggest a butterfly. A number of my pictures started in just that way. Little upright leaves

of nettle suggested trees or bushes, so I wondered if I could make a landscape. This sent me hunting through my leaf collection for some material to use as hills: I finally decided on old tulip leaves. I'm lucky if I find my complete picture, but if not, I put what I have aside in a separate folder, label it 'landscape' and on my next collecting trip to country or garden look specially for the other shapes I need.

Collecting material for pictures makes one look really closely at plants, not only for the obvious beauty, but also as material with which to 'draw'. A leaf that an insect has holed, sometimes with a marvellous regularity, doesn't just mean 'I must get out the sprayer' but also 'I wonder how that would

*A simple design using grass and bracts. Both the violet and red varieties of* Anemone pulsatilla *(Pasque flower) press to a rather muddy shade, but the lovely bracts behind the flowers are worth looking for. The grasses used here are foreign and only to be found in shops selling dried plant material. They were coiled in the pressing papers with the aid of little bits of sticky tape.*

*When it came to sticking the material to the background, only the faintest suggestion of adhesive was used, too much and the minute hairs stick together making it obvious where the glue has been applied. In this kind of design, where the beauty of the material is of utmost importance, this would detract a great deal from the finished effect.*

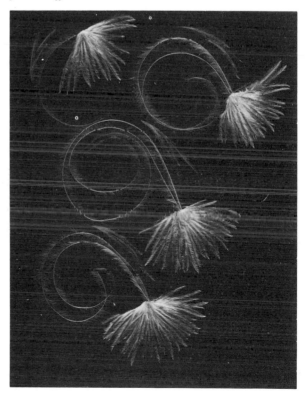

look with a coloured background showing through?' 'Lacy' might be the appropriate word. In fact, when you become interested you will be gathering what to others will seem the most unlikely material, but cleaned and pressed it can have the most interesting possibilities. With this new awareness, country walks will take on an extra pleasure, so long as you remember to take a paper bag with you. A word of warning, although possibly only the heads will be used in a picture, do pick flowers with a length of stem, for they may need a reviving drink before being pressed.

It must be years now since I came home from walking the dog without something in my hand. Even in winter the skeletons of grasses after the seeds have fallen are wonderfully delicate. Living in the country I am particularly lucky in having a wide selection of plant material to choose from, though I nearly lost my supply last year when our village decided to enter the tidy village competition and all my weeds were cropped! Fortunately, they are persistent.

All sorts of plants can provide one with suitable material. Some of the tiny wild flowers, cinquefoil, nipplewort and the little rosy flowers of crane's bill, are so useful for miniature pictures and give a delicate touch to an arrangement of the larger garden flowers. And that patch of daisies in the lawn will be given a reprieve, especially if the flowers have pink edges.

After a time you will be wanting a wider selection of flowers than those in your own garden, especially if it is a small town garden. This is when you will find your friends and neighbours coming to your aid. Once they know of your hobby they will very likely knock on your door as mine have done in the past, sometimes holding a bloom and saying 'This has just come out, it's such a lovely colour I thought you might like it', or 'We are going on holiday, would you like to do some dead-heading while we're away?' Knowing full well that the heads you take will be far from dead, but nothing is lost for them as it will encourage further blooms for their return.

It is quite exciting after you have been pressing for some time to meet a new flower. How shall it be pressed? Will it hold its colour? On the whole a surprising amount of colour is retained in petals if the flowers are picked when they are in their prime and the petals dry, and then pressed as soon as possible. The colours do mellow after some years, but if the picture is well designed it is just as pleasing as when you first made it—sometimes even gaining in interest as the tones become more subtle. A vase of flowers thoughtfully arranged can in later years look lovely in shades of gold, brown, black and cream, highlighted with touches of the original colours.

Quite a lot of the flowers and leaves used in the illustrations in this book are three to four years old. As a general rule flowers which last well on the growing plant will press and keep their colour well, while those which are fleeting, such as tradescantia and day lily (hemerocallis), lose most of their colour quickly, some pressing so thin as to be difficult to handle. Yellow petals, I find, keep their colour most consistently, also the blue of the delphinium, and most coloured leaves alter only slightly.

Press anything that has a good substance, interesting shape or veining. Try some flowers from that special bouquet you have been given and delight the giver with your picture. Use the language of flowers: eschscholzia – sweetness, alyssum – worth beyond beauty, fennel – worthy of all praise. Find four-leaved clovers, make them into a posy picture and give it to someone dear to you.

At very little cost, though I admit quite a lot of time, you can make these pictures and, once started, I think I can promise a new interest in everything that grows, a hobby dealing only with beautiful things which give a feeling of tranquillity in these rather harassing times. It isn't necessary to be able to draw or paint, you are not faced with blank canvas and uninspiring tubes of paint, the materials are beautiful to begin with; they will help you to place them by the curve of their own shape and by the way you saw them growing.

So make flower pictures first, and later, when you realise all the shapes there are in Nature, you will see birds' wings in the shape of a leaf and, with a picture of a bird to help, you will find that you can make a very pleasing copy. If yours turns out to be a rather exotic, fantasy bird, so much the better. I once did an extraordinary bird carrying a daisy chain in its beak, a kind that no ornithologist ever saw, but it made a picture that greatly appealed to children.

So collect your flowers, press them, and set your imagination to work, and I know you will spend many enjoyable hours with this fascinating hobby.

## How Pressing is Done

### Preparing the Material

As dampness can cause blotching, pick all flowers and leaves when they are dry, and only press material which is in perfect condition. Bruising on flowers is not always noticeable but will show up after pressing. Bruised flowers should be discarded as soon as they are noticed.

Pick some wild flowers as well as the cultivated ones; but take great care not to pick rare ones, rather it is the really weedy kinds that are always being chopped down, such as rose bay willow herb and Queen Anne's lace (also known as wild parsley), that I find so very useful.

It is possible, with enough pressure, to get a thick flower nearly flat but the result won't be very pleasing, a clean-pressed look is the aim rather than a squashed look!

**Flowers with many petals** Flowers such as chrysanthemums and dahlias, which have many petals, are taken to pieces, each petal being pressed separately. Do not discard any twisted or distorted ones as these help to give a natural movement to the finished flower.

Smaller flowers, such as kerria, which have many petals of a rather indefinite shape press successfully if the petals are reduced by about half—or until the green base starts to be visible.

**Flowers with thick centres** Some flowers, such as clematis, hellebore and anemone, have thick centres caused by their prominent stamens. These can be removed altogether with the thumbnail, or reduced to just a fringe of stamens. The hellebore is a good flower to practise on as it is firm in texture. (This, by the way, is one of my favourites for pressing as it keeps its subtle colouring indefinitely.)

If, after pressing, the centre where the stamens were removed is unsatisfactory, perhaps a bad colour, it can be covered with a floret of Queen Anne's lace or fennel, for these are very thin when pressed and so add little bulk to the flower.

**Flowers with a tubular shape** Tubular flowers, such as salpiglossis, nicotiana, and the larger vincas, can be cut just below where the petals join and pressed as a circle. Do not worry about the hole in the middle— this will decrease a bit in the pressing and can be covered with a centre as previously suggested. Smaller tubular flowers, such as polyanthus and auricula, can be treated in the same way. They can also be pressed sideways after removing the calyx, half of which can be replaced when making the picture.

**Collective flower heads** Some plants, such as heuchera, have numerous small flowers on a main stem. The upper three or four inches is thin enough to press complete with the stem, but if all the flowers are left on the result will be rather untidy. The answer is to thin them out so that there is much less overlapping and small side stems can be cut out altogether. Press separately some of the little individual flowers that have been removed, as you may want to add one or two here and there, perhaps to emphasise a curve.

**Half-open flowers and buds** Flowers which haven't opened completely or are still in bud should be halved before pressing, not only to make two out of one but also to remove the bulky centre, leaving only half the petals, calyx and stem. This can be done with a razor blade fixed in a handle, but with practice a more satisfactory job can be done by using the two thumbnails. A half-opened flower, as it is held by the stem, will often incline its head very slightly forwards or downwards and the thumbnails should be placed on

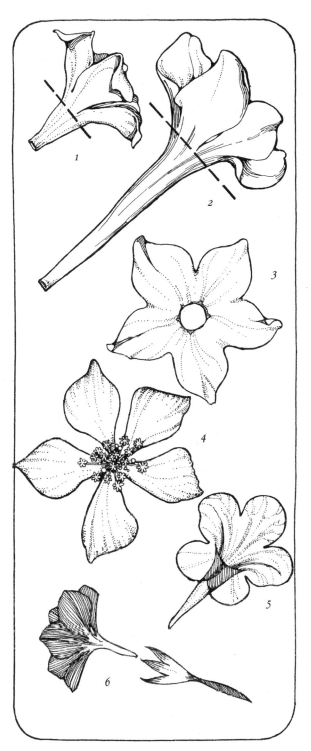

*Flowers with a tubular shape can be pressed open after cutting the head from the tube 1, 2, 3. An added centre is optional 4. Small flowers can be pressed whole 5, or polyanthus can be pressed sideways 6.*

the back of the neck of the flower, which then generally parts evenly through the centre. The stem will also split and this causes it to curve in a pleasing shape.

**Other flower shapes** You will continually be coming across new flowers; don't always press them in the most obvious way, which is usually open faced. Experiment a bit, press them looking sideways; take some completely to pieces; in others, reduce the number of petals; look at the backs, sometimes the best colouring is here.

Press all the little parts that go to make up a flower, for example, if you have a pot of *Primula malacoides*

*Remove the bulky centres from daisies and similar flowers so that they will press flat 1. The backs can be attractive 2. Side views with most of the stamens removed 3.*

(fairy primrose), a very popular pot plant, there is more to it than just the flowers. Where faded flowers have dropped you will notice a little green star is left. This is the calyx and it, too, can be pressed. It is slightly tubular at the base so with scissors cut the tube away to make pressing easier. The white powder on it (farina) makes it very effective as a star when it is placed on a dark background (see the picture on page 68). It can also be used as a centre for delicate flowers. And the little stalk with the lower half of the cut calyx still attached makes a butterfly antenna.

**Leaves** These may be picked at all times of the year, from the newly opened ones in spring, which on many trees and shrubs have a bronze or purplish tinge before assuming their full green colour, and this often deepens in pressing, to the many tints of autumn.

Leaves generally give the line to a flower picture. Perfectly symmetrical leaves on straight stems will result in a stiff look, so search for those which have a suggestion of a curve, even if it's only at the tip, such as many of the leaves on the shrub *Kerria japonica*. Make sure they are clean, no insects on the back and no blemishes. If the leaf has a prominent mid-rib, reduce some of it with a razor blade before pressing.

New shoots on many shrubs, such as symphoricarpos (snowberry) and chaenomeles (cydonia) with three to five small leaves, can be persuaded into a curve for pressing by holding them in one hand and gently shaping with the other. Being new and pliable they will stay in shape and press flat.

Silver and grey leaves such as those of the artemisias and cinerarias, which are so popular just now, can be pressed and relied on to keep their colour indefinitely, looking superb on a dark background.

Leaves from wild plants such as are found in the vetch family have the most interesting shapes plus little curly tendrils. Leave the tendrils on as they often give just the desired lift to a picture.

Prettily shaped leaves will add lightness and a delicate touch to smaller pictures, so look for *Dicentra formosa* (individual leaflets), *Acer palmatum dissectum* and thalictrums.

On the whole, most leaves will press satisfactorily, some exceptions being succulent leaves and those which have no interest other than their bright green colour, for this will fade. If the pressure has not been even, some of the leaves—perhaps on the outer edges of the pressing paper—may look a little wrinkled. You have nothing to lose by trying to smooth them out with a cool iron. This works in most cases, so long as the moisture has been pressed out of the leaf first.

**Notes on pressing**

**Materials required** Newspapers; blotting paper; hardboard; house bricks; scissors—a good sharp pair with long blades such as hairdressers use and a small pair with curved blades.

As can be seen from this list, nothing expensive or complicated in the way of materials is needed. A trouser press can be used and has a wide pressing area but I keep mine for things that need long pressing. Fresh plant material needs to be put under pressure as soon as possible, and this is quicker and simpler if it is just slipped under two house bricks instead of having to unscrew the trouser press, arrange the material and screw up again at the right pressure. In fact, I find the bricks give the most satisfactory even pressure.

**Method of pressing** Place three large double sheets of newspaper together and fold into four, then cut two pieces of blotting paper to the same size (roughly 12 in. by 8 in.). Place one piece of blotting paper in the fold of the newspaper and lay the plant material on this. Do not mix flowers or leaves of a different thickness or pressing will be uneven.

When arranging the material nothing should overlap or an impression will be left, and if flowers or leaf tips incline upwards, turn them face down. Always allow sufficient room for stems bearing a number of small flowers to spread out during pressing.

Cover the material with the second piece of blotting paper and close the newspaper. A piece of hardboard of roughly the same size is placed on top to create an even pressure, and the weight supplied by two house bricks. It helps to arrange and press the material in piles of about one foot high.

Do not be tempted to open the papers for at least ten days as the petals may start to roll up if lifted from the paper too soon. Once this has happened it can be very difficult, or impossible if they are very thin, to flatten them out again.

The quicker the flowers dry out the more colour is retained, so change the papers of thicker petals, such as lilies, and always keep pressings in a warm, dry place.

*By rolling the blotting paper gently over the flowers the material for pressing is not dislodged.*

## Coping with Seaweed

Some of the seaweeds found on our beaches are infinitely delicate and well worth the little trouble needed to preserve them. Suitable seaweeds will be found as small tangles of red, green, cream and dark brown. Collect some of each colour in a plastic bag, but only the tiny ones; the thick, brown, leathery ones are too bulky to press. Wash the seaweed to get rid of the sand and thin out or divide extra bushy pieces. In a bowl of clean water submerge a piece of cartridge or similar paper. It should be larger than the estimated area of the seaweed. Float the seaweed on to

BELOW
*The background for this sea scene is painted with water colour – just faintly – on pale green card. This is only an impression of an underwater scene, not an attempt to depict what is actually found there. I like to think there may be 'herbaceous' borders full of mysterious flowers, like this one.*

*Skeletonised physalis has the right texture for delicate flowers whilst honeysuckle buds make a vaguely sea anemone flower shape. Fine fennel foliage bends with the movement of the water, with dark green and black seaweeds giving depth near the spear thistle leaf. Floating on the right is half a horseradish leaf. This supports green and red seaweeds, some with added curls of bryony. Oplismenus leaves make good darting fish; scuttling before them are two little shapes taken from the centre of passion flowers.*

this and with a small brush spread out the little fronds to an attractive shape–not stiffly upright but with a curved floating line.

Carefully remove the paper from the water with the seaweed in position, tilting the paper slightly to allow surplus water to run off. Place a piece of dry blotting paper on top, and put the whole between thick newspapers under a couple of bricks. (Don't add to other piles of pressed items because of the damp.) Leave for two or three days then change both the pressing papers. It is best if these are carefully rolled off, since as the seaweed is rather sticky it adheres closely to the paper and is likely to break if the papers are lifted off. Leave again for about a week when the seaweed may be handled easily.

Seaweed pictures should keep their colours for many years. Certainly, I have seen some old Victorian pictures which have altered very little in colour.

# Designs for Pictures

On the whole I think that subjects chosen for pictures should have some affinity with plant life, such as posies, flower arrangements in containers, nature pictures of birds and butterflies, and other insects, which are always associated with flowers. Sea pictures and landscapes making use of seaweed and underwater 'flowers' are also good subjects, see pages 55 and 73.

I would not want, for instance, to try a portrait in plant material, or a room interior, unless it's a greenhouse! Too much trimming would be needed and I think there would be little point; there are better mediums for such subjects. So keep to flowery subjects and the results will be more pleasing.

Do start with some idea of how you want the finished picture to look. It will show if thought and planning have gone into it, for it will have balance and finish and pleasing detail, just as it will show if only a haphazard arrangement is made of leaves and flowers that happen to be at hand, pretty in themselves but not arranged to best advantage.

I think these pressed flower pictures can be quite lovely, and very satisfying if made well, so though it does take time, do look through your collection for the best possible shape or colour for the design or picture you have in mind. Naturally an artistic leaning helps but you are halfway there with the basic shapes of the flowers and leaves.

Inspiration for design can be obtained from many sources. Plant life has always been copied in the arts–wood carving, architecture, decorative plaster work (especially ceilings), lace making and painting–with the most beautiful results.

*A pair of quite small pictures with similar material used in each. Both have branches of vine leaves at the top with berries of* Berberis thunbergii *leaves. Pale blue delphinium petals, with deep blue* Salvia horminum *added, make the matching flowers.*

*The moth/butterfly in the left-hand picture has a body of an autumnal yellow spiraea leaf, with small curly chrysanthemum petals (taken from the centre of the flower). The brownish-crimson wings are made from the brilliant scarlet bracts of poinsettia, with dark grey willow leaves behind.*

*The somewhat exotic bird has a head and beak of a berberis leaf. I was pleased with the topknot, which was found at the base of a dahlia after picking all the petals off; it is semi-transparent with purple edges. The wings are of willow, on a body of wild crab apple. The intricate tail starts with a dark red leaf of acer and curving from it are light and dark chrysanthemum petals, rose bay willow herb curls and spiraea leaves. Both moth and bird include little bunches of fine, silky, green grass bought from the florist–these help to give a suggestion of flight.*

Try to copy a flower picture that you like. Probably you won't have exactly the same shaped flowers but if enough material has been prepared you will be able to select something similar or contrive it with loose petals and leaves.

Possibly you will be content making only flower pictures and there is endless scope, from simple posies tied with a grass ribbon to copies of those beautiful old Dutch paintings, and remember that a dark background gives a lovely period look. The fact that some flowers fade to a lighter tone can be used to advantage on such a background, but avoid those listed on page 93 as becoming almost transparent. This quality can be exploited with the right choice of coloured ground but it takes a bit of trial and error.

## Simple Designs

If you are keen to get started and do not want to wait for the initial fading or changing of petal colour, simple modern designs can be made using the flowers as soon as they can be handled, that is in about two or three weeks. The picture could be made to match your furnishing, for no doubt you will be re-decorating by the time the colour has lost its freshness. But as long as the design is good and well balanced the picture, though eventually changing, will still be pleasing.

A simple embroidery pattern can start you off, perhaps a square or circular design. Decide on the predominant flowers, the secondary ones, and the leaves, do not try to copy the design exactly or try to make the picture more realistic, but just make a pleasing, balanced pattern. Move the material about until you feel happy with the result. Get to know the possibilities of the material, the shapes that complement each other, the colour range and different textures. You will see that heavy leaves can swamp the delicacy of flowers, so find lighter, more graceful ones, not too many, just enough to underline the importance of the flowers.

## Advanced Designs

For designs on more classical lines which will take more time and effort, it is best to wait until after the initial fading or colour changes of the plant material, about eight to twelve weeks. This will ensure a good colour balance and that the best colour background is chosen.

There are some lovely examples of suitable designs to be found—books on old lace will contain many that use superb flower shapes, curving lilies with backward-curving leaves embracing other flowers in their curves, which in turn curl and burst into a fan of tiny flowers, the whole design having movement and growth.

Plaster work in some of our lovely old houses and stately homes has often given me a clue for a design, perhaps only the basic line, an elongated S shape used diagonally, a curving branch heavy with drooping fruit, twists and trails of tiny flowers peeping out between larger ones.

The antique shops with their lovely painted porcelain will make you get out paper and pencil, not to see if you can afford the piece but to draw quickly a rough impression of that unusual way of placing the flower which makes the body of the vase look even rounder than it is.

You won't necessarily want to copy other ideas all the time, and in any case your different material will see to it that the design is original, even though the basic idea came from elsewhere. Inspiration will come from simply using the flowers and leaves, knowing the effects that you can get with them and, because they are so lovely, wanting to use them to best advantage. With this aim alone you can hardly fail to make lovely, satisfying floral designs.

## Imaginative Pictures

Having made many pictures of either floral designs or traditional subjects such as landscapes, vases of

flowers etc., sometimes I find when I have some extra beautiful plant material to use that I want it to dominate the picture somehow, the subject to come second to the visual beauty of the petals and leaves.

To do this effectively the most important thing is that the material must be immaculate and have an interesting or pleasing texture. There should be very little trimming so that there is nothing contrived about the effect; the idea is to show just how lovely leaves and petals can be without relying on a subject that is generally accepted as pleasing. It is possible that the material itself will suggest the best use, little imagination was needed for the design of the picture on page 68, the silver-green sheen on the leaves suggested moonlight to me and the design just asked for a dark background.

A little more thought was needed in the use of the leaves and petals in the top picture on page 72; this illustrates a rather restrained use of material, just enough to suggest the subject, to make the viewer look more closely at what is there and appreciate the lovely lines and textures.

## Pictures for a Child's Room

Children find fascination in ordinary things used in a special way. To see familiar flowers and seedheads

*A dark background was chosen for this imaginary spider's web—it gives the touch of mystery that this kind of subject needs. The feathery grasses, which came from Provence, seemed the right kind of delicate airy material to try to make into a web. It wasn't easy as they were springy and had a very definite curve to which they returned every time I tried to alter their shape. Eventually I found that if they were damped a little, then pressed again into the desired shape, they could be used. Great care must be taken to stick them without any adhesive showing, and I used little weights to hold the web in position after applying only the slightest touch of adhesive.*

*Single petals of a spider chrysanthemum radiate from the centre of the web and part of a seedhead of hogweed, softened by bleaching and pressed flat, draws all the pieces to the central point. Not a distinct spider, or a definite web, but enough to suggest one that is lightly attached to delicate grasses and looks as though it might drift away at any moment with the butterflies.*

*Choosing petals with silky textures and interesting veining to make the butterflies was an enjoyable task. Suitable plants include alstroemeria, delphinium, eschscholzia,* Helleborus orientalis, *hypericum, malope,* Pelargonium *Carrisbrooke,* Rosa mundi *and tulip. Honeysuckle buds make good bodies with the transparent parts of shepherd's purse seed cases for antennae.*

gain the importance of a framed picture adds another dimension to their appreciation of the attractive things in Nature. If the pictures are made of especially appealing material such as silky or downy leaves that they would like to touch, or fluffy seedheads, they will be doubly pleasing to them.

Simple flower pictures look well in a child's room, but ideally the subject should be gay or amusing. A fantastic bird carrying a daisy chain in its beak found great favour. A cat's head, odd though it may seem, with ears and fur collar of autumn-bronzed silver weed, big yellow round flowers for its cheeks, a cotoneaster leaf nose and yellow oval dahlia petal eyes with elongated berberis leaves for the irises, was most intriguing.

But favourite of all has been a woolly rabbit. Lovely leaves of *Salvia argentea* were pressed because I couldn't resist their silky, downy texture, though at the time I had no idea what use they would be, for they were obviously too heavy to blend with petals. It was so natural to stroke them when opening the papers to see if they were pressing well, that a furry animal seemed the right choice. Ears of senecio, which shows fine white edges, were pressed to go with the head and body of salvia, a pussy willow tail soon followed. Limbs were made of *Alchemilla alpina* showing the green side; the paw, which was holding an umbrella, showed the silvery reverse side.

Not wanting—or being able to give him a face—it had to be a back view, which led to the reason why he was sitting there, looking at something perhaps? I finally decided that he was just patiently waiting under a willow leaf umbrella for the shower of mimosa blossom to pass. He squashes little flowers with his furry bottom, but grasses and daisies on either side come to no harm.

Ideas will come for children's pictures just from looking at their books. For instance, I'm sure you have some 'owl's feathers' in your collection!

## Landscape Pictures

Scenes of the countryside are very interesting to make, testing your ingenuity and imagination in seeing leaves in quite a different role from their usual one of enhancing flowers. The aim is for the picture to have the look of a water colour—a restrained, delicate wash of colour with the minimum of material that gives an impression of hills, fields, water and trees rather than an intricate collage of much detail, which, although cleverly chosen, must obscure the clean lines which give perspective to a landscape picture.

Once you have decided to try a landscape, hills, grassy banks, bushes and lower vegetation will be needed, and you should start to look at plants with these things in mind. Some will be found among the material already pressed, others will have to be searched for and prepared. The fact that a lot of the

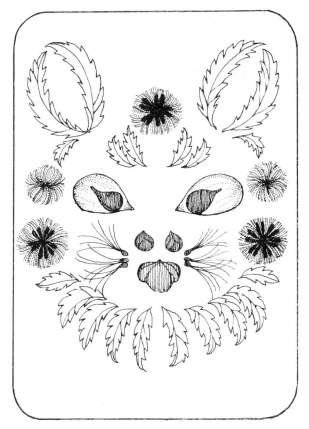

green colour fades from the leaves is not very important. When they have been pressed and the initial fading has taken place, it will be found that touches of green remain, often streaking a leaf very effectively. These can be used to emphasise the curve of a hill. Most of the shades found in Nature can be seen among pressed leaves and other plant material, for example cream, bronze, many shades of brown and purplish tones. Leaf veins, too, can be relied on to accentuate a curved shape, and variegation can be used to advantage.

**Hills** Old tulip leaves make good hills, fading to pale gold with dark brown shading, and with veining in shallow curves along the length of the leaf.

Half hosta leaves are also effective, particularly the variegated varieties which have distinct shading just as you would wish it to be—darker at the base (near the ground) and fading to merge with the sky at the outer curve.

**Smooth grassy banks** The 'flowers' (spathes) of the wild arum, sometimes called cuckoo-pint, are very useful for making grassy banks. Collect them when they first unfurl and look like green glass; they become very thin when pressed but are not difficult to handle. Collect again when they are mature; these will be thicker and darker in colour, often tinged effectively

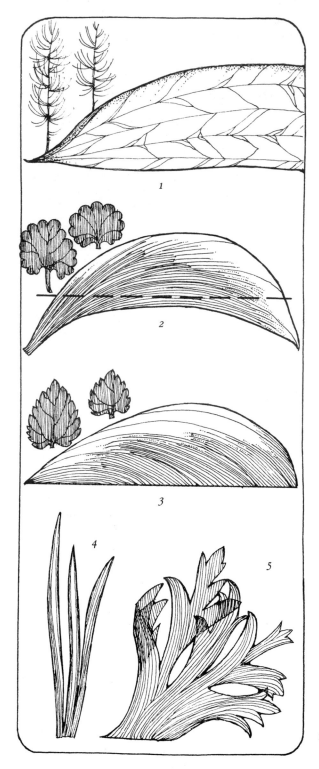

*Landscape material: wild arum spathe with fennel trees 1; part of hosta leaf with nepeta bushes 2, or dead nettle 3; crocus 4; anemone leaf 5.*

with purple, just the shade an artist would choose when shading, particularly a Scottish artist.

To press wild arums, cut off the bulbous base and the spadix (the stem which will later bear orange berries) will drop out. A cut is then made up the centre of the spathe, resulting in two grassy banks with flat (cut) bases and sloping tops (natural edges). In the pressing the very tips will probably fold and twist just a fraction. Don't try to do anything about this, it looks just right when it becomes the base of a bank.

Press the spathes for about six to eight weeks. The thinner ones may need to have the blotting paper rolled off them as they are inclined to be sticky when first put in the pressing papers and adhere closely. However, once off they handle quite easily.

**Trees** Trees are an important part of any landscape. For those farthest away in the distance small side pieces of feathery fennel are admirable. I find this keeps a good suggestion of green colour, and cream and bronze pieces can also be found in the older, lower leaves. Coming nearer in the picture leaves of nettle, often having touches of purple, make very good tree shapes with their serrated edges. Collect all sizes so that a suggestion of depth can be given to the landscape by using them diminishing in size with the distance.

**Bushes** The variegated form of *Nepeta glechoma* makes such pretty little bushes with its scalloped edges. *Tolmiea menziesii*, a hardy plant which is often grown in pots, is another one to use. The leaves are slightly downy and press to a beautiful pale almond green on one side with pinkish-grey on the other. Really minute leaves can also be found sitting on the backs of the larger ones (hence tolmiea's nickname, the pick-a-back plant).

**Other Vegetation** Little bunches of small grass blades can be used as rushes. But even better are crocus leaves. Many of these are striped with white, which emphasises an upright shape.

Sections cut from the leaves of some of the scented pelargoniums, *P. filicifolium* is a good choice, will provide blunted branch shapes. These placed to suggest pieces of a fallen tree look particularly well near water.

Where a little weight is needed, perhaps in the foreground, tiny touches of moss (pressed *Alchemilla mollis* flowers) can be added. This should not be overdone; a little near the base of a tree, or to mark the side of a path, is sufficient.

**Birds** Some birds flying high will help with the atmosphere of a landscape. These can be made remarkably simply from leaves of *Anthriscus sylvestris* (Queen Anne's lace, wild parsley). In May and June before these plants get chopped down in the general wayside tidying up, leaves can be found about halfway up the stems of a deep purplish-crimson colour, which turns darker when pressed. It is usually the first two pairs of leaflets nearest the main stem which have the best shapes. Cut them, keeping the pair of leaflets – one on either side of the stem – intact. To do this a tiny portion of the stem is included with the leaves by cutting just above and just below where the two leaves meet. Often, the leaflet on one side is inclined at a higher angle than the other. This is to be desired, as it suggests a bird in flight more realistically than a pair of leaflets which are perfectly balanced. Cut three or four pairs of diminishing sizes and you have a flight of birds.

**Butterflies and bees** These are simple to make and suitable petals include those of colchicum and tulip, both silky in texture when pressed, and alstroemeria and *Rosa mundi* which have pretty markings. The annual malope, which has veining fanning out from the base, is especially useful for suggesting a wing.

Two petals will make the outspread wings of a butterfly, one on each side of a honeysuckle bud body. A second pair, either similar or harmonising in colour, can be added to make a larger butterfly – it is fascinating to try out different combinations. For a side view, one petal is placed over another, partly obscuring it, and the body positioned over the base of the petals.

A dark gazania or velvety brown rudbeckia petal provides a body for a bee with little stripes of small curly yellow chrysanthemum petals found in the centre of the flower. Pale yellow zinnia petals make good bee wings as the backs have faint veining.

The antennae for both butterflies and bees can be made from a range of material: stamens of fuchsias or lilies; tiny narrow petals such as those found in an opening bud of calceolaria; transparent discs from shepherd's purse; the thin little stalks with the base of a calyx still attached from a plant such as *Primula malacoides*.

*Birds can be made from Queen Anne's lace.*

# How Pictures are Made

**Materials required** Mounting card in black, white and a range of colours; transparent adhesive such as Uhu; rubber-based adhesive such as Copydex; scissors with straight and curved blades; knife with a rounded tip; small knitting needle with knob on the end; medium-sized artist's paintbrush; tissues.

Having decided on the kind of picture you want to make you should prepare two identical pieces of card, one on which to practise the design, the other on which to make the picture.

Move the chosen flowers about on the practice card, using either the knife blade or the paintbrush – whichever you prefer to handle – until satisfied with the result. The flowers are then transferred, one by one, and stuck down on the other piece of card. This is easier than trying to stick the design as a whole on the first card, some pieces are sure to get moved as you work, also the practice card will very likely get marked, and a beautiful clean look adds much to the finished picture.

For flower arrangement pictures, begin with the vase, basket or stems. If a design has a definite important 'line' such as the curve of a bird (see page 68), begin with this.

### Sticking

For petals and leaves use the rubber-based adhesive. For baskets and pots made from rushes a clear adhesive is more suitable.

**Stems** Apply little dots of adhesive with the knitting needle point to the tip of the stem and at intervals of roughly $\frac{3}{4}$ in. along it, leaving the end you are holding. Place the stem in position, put blotting paper over it and apply a little pressure with the hand. The blotting paper is used because the slightest perspiration from the fingers can mark the card, especially on dark grounds. When firmly in place, put a little adhesive on the upper side of the knife tip and slide this under the unglued end of the stem. Press this also – the knob end of the knitting needle is useful for pressing tips.

**Leaves and petals** A little adhesive is applied to the base of the single leaf or petal, which is then stuck in place. Balancing the piece to be stuck across the knife and offering it to the picture is a good way to get it at just the right angle. If need be, as only the base is glued, it can often be swivelled round to a better position before any pressure is applied.

**Complete flowers** Flowers which have been pressed without removing all the petals need only a blob of glue in the centre.

**Stamens** Single stamens, such as those used for butterfly antennae and for making up fuchsia-type

61

flowers, may look difficult to handle, but are quite simple if stuck in the same way as a stem—one end at a time.

**Grasses** These need just a little glue here and there on the thicker portions. They will keep their nice airy look if not appearing to be stuck down too well.

Should some adhesive accidentally get on to part of the background, use a tissue to remove it, gently working in one direction only. The rubber-based kind can be rolled off cleanly, the clear kind is best dabbed two or three times with a clean area of tissue. If all fails—will a butterfly fit in?

## FRAMING

When the picture is quite finished, place a piece of blotting paper over the whole area, then a piece of glass or hardboard on top and weight it with a couple of books. Leave for about two days to dry thoroughly and to flatten any lifting material.

If you should require the effect of a mount, perhaps a coloured one to pick out and emphasise a colour in the picture (see page 77), then the mount must be placed behind the picture. This can be achieved by fastening the picture with a little glue in position on a sheet of the chosen colour, so that when framed the plant material will be in contact with the glass. It is important that the picture is not recessed in a cut out mount as is usual because this would prevent the necessary pressure of the glass on the plant material, which will lift after a time and lose its clean outline.

The picture should be backed with hardboard and nailed as firmly as possible. Choose the frame carefully as the right one can greatly enhance a picture. For example, a Japanese-type arrangement, or a landscape, looks attractive in a narrow dark frame. A fresh modern flower picture or design is best in either natural or white painted wood, and an 'old master', of course, looks at home in an antique gilt frame.

### Hanging

Some pictures, especially those of the seed-bearing parts of plants, retain their colour indefinitely even in a fairly bright light. To keep colour in flower pictures for as long as possible, avoid hanging them in bright sunlight.

I have yet to test the long-term effect of bleaching plant material; I think it is possible that in time they may take on an ivory tone, which could be very pleasing. So far, though, in eighteen months there has been no change.

Generally speaking, keep pictures away from damp atmospheres and from very bright sunlight, which, after all, fades most things in time.

## PAINTED BACKGROUNDS

Only three of the illustrations used in this book have some added colour—a suggestion of a painted outline on the background. This is a fairly recent experiment of mine which, I think, should not be overdone. It should be used very sparingly to suggest the atmosphere (as in the sea scene on page 55) and then only if it cannot be done in a satisfactory way using plant material.

In the picture of flowers under a dome it would have been possible to outline a dome shape with long grass stalks but highlighting with paint would still have been needed to get any effect of glass. It seemed best to keep to paint for the dome and actual plant material for the inside.

At one stage I had thought of painting a plain white vase on to a background and decorating this with flowers, like a piece of Worcester or some such similar porcelain. But then I tried making the vase outline with leaves and though the background colour showed through I was reasonably pleased with the result and abandoned the idea of a painted vase.

*Trying to buy a glass dome to cover a delicate ornament led to this picture. The antique shops wouldn't sell an empty one, they all contained stuffed birds or artificial flowers. I tried to get something of this artificial quality in these flowers by using dried seedy material. In fact, almost everything—except for a few leaves—is from the seed-bearing part of the plants. In some cases only half of the thickness is used so that the picture remains flat, although it has a three dimensional look.*

*A good impression of a dome using plant material was beyond me. I tried fine grass stems for the outline but eventually decided to paint it with water colour. A dark greenish-grey background was the most suitable for the white water colour to show up well and give the effect of a glass dome. There is also some darker shading painted in on the left side of the dome and around the base. The 'wooden' stand is made from three leaves of* Sisyrinchium striatum, *whose older leaves in autumn change to brown then nearly black without their firm texture deteriorating. Half a large leaf of* Plantago major rubrifolia *makes the vase; the base is part of a smaller leaf inverted.*

*None of the material inside the dome is painted; all the delicate sprays around the edges are various very fine grasses and winter skeletons of empty seed cases. The largest, delicate-looking flower is made of layers of skeletonised physalis with a centre taken from a passion flower. To the right, and a little above, is a flower made from circular honesty outer seed cases with coils of passion flower tendrils placed on each and an intricate astrantia flower for a centre. Physalis again, with white parts of acanthus, is used for the flower shown in side view above this. To the left, the centre taken from a hypericum holds thistledown in place and next to it is a coltsfoot seedhead, which also needs a centre to keep it intact. The clustered silky textured flowers above are opened seed cases of eucomis and fluffy, manageable dryas is seen at the top.*

63

Certainly there are no rules for making these pictures, except the one I have made for myself—not to stick anything on them that is not plant material. If the painting is overdone one will tend to wonder where it stops, for example, is that shading done with a dark leaf or is it painted? This would be a pity if you had put in some rather clever work and got the shaded effect with plant material. Also, it would be defeating the object of making pictures with flowers in the first place.

I think the only acceptable occasions for painting would be along the following lines: to trace a suggestion of a stone niche for an old Dutch type of flower picture; to outline a table top to stop a vase 'floating'; and to provide a watery background for seaweed pictures. These add greatly to the effect achieved from the plant material itself.

The only paint I have used is water colour; the thick texture of oils would be out of place with delicate flowers, which, if they were placed on it, might suffer a detrimental effect, such as the oil showing through

OPPOSITE PAGE, TOP LEFT

*A flower picture, in the traditional manner, which includes auriculas, my favourite flowers to grow, even though when used for pressing their brilliant colouring is much subdued. The vase is a thin colchicum leaf picked in May when it had changed to this golden-brown shade. It was chosen for its rounded shape and silky sheen, which was accentuated by ironing it with a cool iron. The trail of heuchera and the small dark leaves which are placed on the vase do not make for undesirable bulkiness as the colchicum leaf is wafer thin.*

*Schizanthus petals make the round deep pink flower touching the vase. Behind it is an auricula, with two more above, still showing the mealy white farina. Next to these is a very dark primula. Deep crimson petals from a regal pelargonium make the largest flower. A flower of purply-pink* Salvia turkestanica *with pointed petals is partly obscuring one of* Helleborus orientalis. *Two red* Salvia splendens, *pressed sideways, are roughly central in position.*

*The flowers around the edge, beginning at the lower left, include yellow ribes, blue verbena, nerine and three chimonanthus. The same pelargonium petals are used for the large dark red flower make the top central bloom. Next come two sprays made up with the tiny bell-shaped flowers of tolmiea. Complete tips taken from* Salvia turkestanica *are further down on the right.*

TOP RIGHT

*An arrangement using only leaves. These still retain much of their autumn colouring which, together with their firm texture, makes a strong design. Back-curling bracken (this is a continuous piece) can be found in autumn and I have used this to make the stem of the container. The larger fronds which outline the shape of the goblet have*

*had the little leaflets removed from one side.*

*Arranged in the goblet are leaves of orange and red amelanchier forming a rosette. A large herbaceous geranium leaf with serrated edges has two smaller darker ones behind. Two oval-shaped* Cotinus coggyria *leaves are on the left of these with a bright red* Viburnum burkwoodii *and two vine leaves around them.* Euphorbia polychroma *leaves change to orange-brown in autumn; their narrow curving shapes make the two 'flowers'. Small new oak leaves surround the flower on the right. Other leaves used include those of berberis, crane's bill, wild carrot and hazel.*

*These pressed leaves can be very brittle so care should be taken to keep them flat. It is safer to slip a knife blade beneath them to pick them up than to lift the edge with the fingers, which might bend them and cause cracking.*

BOTTOM LEFT

*Hydrangeas and hellebores in a vase made of honeysuckle buds. If the idea of the vase appeals to you, do press a lot of buds as some are straighter than others and the sizes vary a great deal. Out of something like eighty buds I only had enough of the right size and shape to make up two vases. The newish buds keep their colour better than mature ones.*

*Toning well with the colour of the honeysuckle are the flowers of hellebore; I have used* Helleborus orientalis *and H. foetidus. Hydrangea florets of various shades fill in the spaces. Starry flowers with coloured edges came from a bulbous plant,* Eucomis bicolor; *when fresh the petals were still this rather pale greenish shade, outlined with purple.*

*Foliage, of quite different texture from the curved smooth petals, is from a fine-leaved artemisia. During summer, some parts of the plant take on this pinkish tone.*

BOTTOM RIGHT

*The fairy lightness of the fluffy seedheads of* Dryas octopetala *led me to the idea of placing little elfish figures gaily swinging from them, making a picture that would delight a child. A dark background is needed to show up the delicacy of the seedheads. Rose bay willow herb seed cases provide the curves for the clouds; smaller pieces under the elves give them movement.*

*To dress the elves, pale gold segments of Chinese lanterns make the baggy trousers, with the backs of* Berberis thunbergii *leaves for the feet—larger ones make the heads. Ivy hats are trimmed with gay hypericum stamen tassels. Autumn finds thin reddish leaves on* Euphorbia polychroma *and these were used for the arms. I was pleased to discover the little hand shapes on* Thalictrum adiantifolium.

*A single silver weed leaf cut up the centre made a body for each of the moths, with wings of* Alchemilla alpina *leaves and antennae of shepherd's purse seed membrane. Little pearl buttons from autumn alyssum plants finished a picture that was fun to do.*

*A pair of pictures using bleached plant material on a black background. The designs are in the restrained Oriental manner, which does justice to beautiful, interesting material.*

*The vase on the right is a partially skeletonised sweet pea leaf, bleached for about two hours. The very fine filigree stems can be found on Artemisia vulgaris in November. If you are not too hasty in clearing the annual Salvia splendens from the garden, the bell-shaped flowers hang on the plant and become a pale golden shade, still quite firm to the touch. All the hanging flowers are made from these, they take one or two days to bleach.*

*Sycamore keys, which make the leaves in both pictures, can take a week to ten days to bleach. Molucella 'shells',*

*which almost become transparent when left on the plant, had a dip in bleach with the most pleasing results and I used pieces of them to make both the butterflies.*

*The larger flowers in the left-hand picture are bleached seed cases of aquilegia. They are too bulky in their natural state, but the segments can be separated and, after bleaching for about one week, they are soft enough to press quite flat. The five hanging flowers on a stem, also the little four-petalled flower, are made from muscari seed cases; about one day will bleach them clean. The tiny, charming bells at the base of the picture are found if little rock campanulas are left so that they skeletonise naturally. They then need only a short dip in bleach to improve their colour.*

66

a thin petal. This would be particularly likely if the paint were not completely dry when the picture was made up.

On the whole I would suggest that you avoid painting for a time—there are so many experiments to make with plant material alone. Although if painting is your first love and flowers come second, you will no doubt go ahead and have a very interesting time, painting vases to put flowers in, branches to put blossom and flowery birds on, even possibly a view into a greenhouse to put flowering pot plants in!

## Pictures Using Bleached Plant Material

Some of the fascinating structure and lovely shapes to be found in plants—especially the seed-bearing parts—can be emphasised by bleaching them to a white or very pale cream shade and using them on a black background. Not all things will bleach satisfactorily, but I keep experimenting because those which are usable are so exquisite. Only perfect material should be chosen so that on close inspection the delicate plant structure is revealed, any signs of shattering and decay and the lovely pristine look will be lost.

**Bleaching** Two teaspoons of ordinary domestic bleach are added to one pint of cold water, and the plant material is soaked in this and inspected every day. As soon as the colour has gone (this is best decided by placing the bleached plant material on a white background) remove the material from the bleach and rinse by leaving in cold water for about half an hour. Gently blot with a tissue to remove excess water, then place in blotting paper and newspaper, changing both until the plant material is quite dry. It will be found that though many things, such as seed cases, are crisp and dry when collected, after bleaching they become soft and can be pressed without difficulty.

I have yet to find out if there is going to be much change in this bleached material when exposed to bright light for some time. As this is a fairly recent experiment, I have only been able to take a note of roughly eighteen months, but so far there has been no change. If time does eventually have any effect I think it will be to give a creamy tone which should be quite acceptable—perhaps to some an improvement!

# *Vases, Pots and Baskets*

Flowers and leaves arranged in designs and patterns can be very attractive, but arranging them in a vase or pot completes the picture. Depending on the kind of flowers chosen, containers can be made from a range of material from some of the delicate trumpet-shaped flowers to leaves, stems and grasses.

## Vases for Small Delicate Pictures

When really flat flowers are used, with little more than the depth of a single petal, suitable vases can be made from various flowers, in particular those which have a tubular or trumpet shape; as in the following.

SALPIGLOSSIS An annual, with flowers in a wide range of colours, some vivid, some beautifully subtle. Most have exquisite veining.

GENTIANA ACAULIS A rock plant with the most vivid blue trumpets. Striking markings—shades of greenish-yellow spotted and striped—are revealed when the throat is exposed, and when made into a vase the most charming pleated effect is formed.

STREPTOCARPUS Pot plants in shades of cherry red, mauve, blue and white. These have recently been improved in size.

FREESIA Available at most times of the year in many colours. Delightful vases with deeply scalloped rims are made from these lovely flowers.

**Making the vases** Choose perfect flowers which are spotless and quite dry. It will be noticed that some of the flowers just mentioned have a slightly shorter side, which is more apparent if the flower is viewed sideways. Some petals, usually two, are not level with the rest. It is here that the flower is opened by cutting from the base to the tip. The result is a vase or fan shape and, because the two sides are shorter, the rim of the vase and the sides are curved prettily. The marking or veining, as it decreases towards the base, emphasises the vase shape.

When pressing the vases the flowers will tend to roll back into their original shape, and it is easier in this case if one folded piece of blotting paper is used instead of two separate pieces. The flowers are placed with the inside surfaces down on the blotting paper, one cut edge being placed and held in the fold while the other hand is used to ensure that the flower stays flat when the blotting paper is being closed. Usually three flowers can be placed along the length of the fold but no others are put in the empty space remaining as they may get dislodged when closing the blotting paper.

As soon as the blotting paper is in position the newspapers are closed and immediately put under pressure.

Honeysuckle buds can be used in a different way to make a pretty vase shape. Collect and press a number of the buds as they vary a lot in length and amount of curve. The deep crimson colour streaks a little after a time but this can add interest to the vase.

Choose eight buds of similar size and two smaller ones. Place two buds as though drawing the outer sides of the vase, then place a matching pair alongside these and repeat the procedure with the next two pairs. The two smaller buds are used in the oval shape that is left in the centre. A bud trimmed to shape can finish the base, or inverted small buds used to make a base that gives the effect of a vase with a waist (see bottom left picture on page 65).

LEFT

The overall faint greenish colour with silky gleaming
highlights, together with the stars and night moths, gives
a touch of moonlight to this design. Kept simple, with no
attempt at detail in the bird shape, it makes an
attractive picture mainly because of the beautiful material.

The silky leaves used for the flowers are the backs of
Alchemilla alpina; these become even more sleek and
shiny after pressing. Petals were removed from pressed
flowers of erigeron and the pretty exposed backs were
added to the base of the alchemilla leaves to make them
more like flower shapes. I collected the little willow
catkins before the centres had a chance to harden, cut them
in half with a sharp knife and pressed them well. The
head and body of the bird are leaves from Cytisus
battandieri, willow leaves make the wings.

Little greenish backs (calyces) of primulas with the
white powder (farina) still on them make effective little
stars. The moth flying among them is made of three small
leaflets of silver weed. The lower moth on the left has

wings of Cytisus battandieri with a body of a piece of
grey artemisia. Both have antennae of part of the seed
case of shepherd's purse.

ABOVE

This is a fairly simple design of the kind that comes to
mind when first starting to make these pictures. A really
pretty vase is a promising start and an opened-up
trumpet of Gentiana acaulis makes this one. I chose
flowers in the same colour range so that the colour balance
would be pleasing and also because if fairly fresh petals
were used the eventual colour changes would be similar
throughout the picture.

The design was made by placing the vase in position
first. Next, the two large flowers directly above; the
flower above these was made of separate petals so that it
was easy to fit in. Others were then added, fitting them in
and gradually building the design outwards. Smaller
flowers soften the outer edges and dark leaves break what
might have been a somewhat solid outline.

## Vases for Larger Pictures

For taller, more substantial looking vases suitable for larger flower pictures, there are a number of leaves which, with a little preparation, will do very well. Look for them among tulips and lily-of-the-valley. Any leaf which has veins curving out from the base in regular lines will most likely be suitable. Avoid those in which the central mid-rib is prominent. Leaves should be collected when all the green colouring has gone, even though they may be creased or folded, because as long as they are quite dry and brown they will take a cool iron, which makes a great improvement to the surface. If too many blotches or tears show up the leaf concerned may not be usable but if half is in good condition, either base to middle or tip to middle, it can be used.

**Making large vases** Cut across the leaf at the widest part, and also across the pointed end so that this is about $\frac{3}{4}$ in. wide. This end will form the base of the vase. A foot for the base is made by cutting a section from the lower half of another similar leaf. This section should start by measuring $\frac{3}{4}$ in. in width (matching the vase base) and widen out to roughly twice that width, making a shaped foot. This can be seen in the picture on page 63 showing an arrangement under a dome.

Alternatively, the pointed base of the leaf can be cut into a gentle curve, and a piece of rush—preferably slightly darker in colour—is placed as a finishing rim at the foot (see top left picture on page 65).

Other suitable leaves can be found among the colchicums. These, although not having the distinct veining which in others helps to suggest a rounded vase, do have a most attractive silky sheen when ironed. This reflects the light at certain angles and I find that I use these leaves often, the pale golden colour blending with any flowers.

Another useful leaf, this time picked before it goes

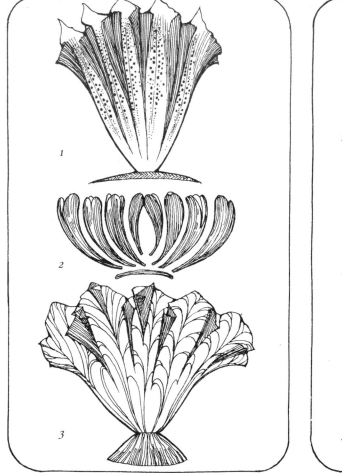

*Vases from gentian 1, honeysuckle 2, salpiglossis 3.*

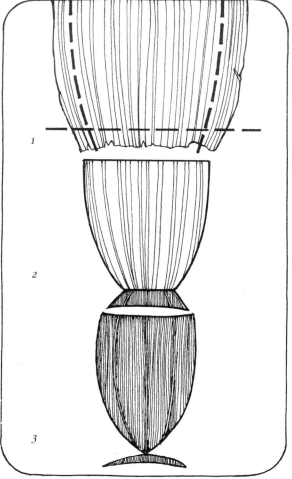

*Vases from fritillaria leaf 1, 2, and plantain 3.*

brown, is obtained from the garden form of the wild plantain, *Plantago major rubrifolia*. The purplish leaves have the most interesting mottling and marbling. By choosing a largish leaf and cutting along the outside of the curving veins, vases of varying sizes may be made, from large ones using the two outer veins as edges, to tallish narrow ones using the two or four central sections. A base is cut from a second leaf as previously described.

Shallow bowls can be made from antholyza leaves; choose those with slight curves and the pleating will help to round the bowl.

## Baskets from Sweet Chestnut Leaves

The colour and texture of these autumn leaves makes a basket with an effective woven look. Choose leaves which are straight and of similar size and the same shade of brown. The reverse side of the leaf is used as the veining is more pronounced.

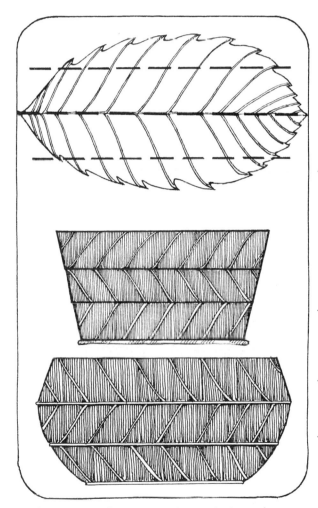

*Making a basket from a sweet chestnut leaf.*

Remove the serrated outer edges of the leaf by cutting in a straight line parallel with the central rib about 1 in. above and below it. Carefully divide the leaf into two by cutting directly under the central rib

PAGE 72, TOP
*A rather restrained use of petals and leaves but showing the beauty of the material to advantage. When making this picture, I had in mind a kind of exotic climbing plant growing up through the undergrowth into the light to be welcomed by butterflies. The plant is anchored there by means of its tendrils. I know the picture doesn't show all this, but it still makes a pleasing design, mostly because the material used is so attractive and in perfect condition.*

*The flowers were made with pale gold delphinium leaves, found low down on the plant, and silky, almost colourless, petals of colchicum which retain just the faintest hint of their original pale purple. Alternating with these are petals of a lily. When fresh these were a brilliant orange but they are even more pleasing now that they are deep rich bronze with orange highlights.*

*Dark crimson tulip petals with interesting touches of yellow and black at the base make the welcoming butterflies. The stems and coils are of brown grass, accentuated with darker strips.*

PAGE 72, BOTTOM
*The bowl for this arrangement was made from the pleated leaves of antholyza, picked in the autumn; the lines of the little pleats help to suggest the curve of the bowl. Dark-coloured leaves of aquilegia, which can often be found in the summer, add shade to the right hand side. Lower centre and far right the leaves are composed of the new growth of sycamore, which presses to this lovely dark colour. A little piece of melilot with tiny yellow flowers adds a highlight here; above are two flowers of Helleborus foetidus with added centres of fennel.*

*I was rather pleased with the way the flower in two shades of purple appears to look down. The brighter petals of dahlia are placed over rose petals which were a deep pink and have faded to this dullish purple. This flower has a small fennel centre. To the right, the flower with tones of dark crimson is made of three petals of clematis. Top right of the dahlia flower is a Lenten hellebore; above this and lower down far right are two eschscholzia poppies pressed sideways. Top centre a flower of a St Brigid anemone, whilst ribes provides the spray of red tubular flowers; two meadow daisies are below. Curving top left are the flowers of larkspur, which keep their colour for a number of years. Coming further down are little white heads of alyssum and the delicate flowers of wild carrot. Three more daisies showing their pink backs are tucked in between two Helleborus corsicus, and lastly a spray of white amelanchier picked in the bud. A few strips of dark rush help to make the bowl appear to be sitting firmly on the ground.*

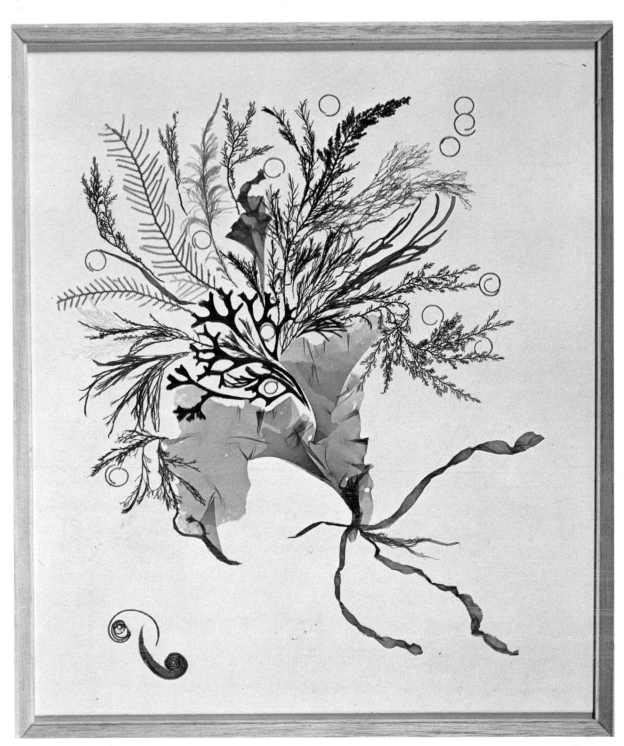

This design is made almost entirely from various seaweeds, except for the bubbles which are from seed cases of rose bay willow herb. It was the ribbon-like green strands and the tissue-wrapping-paper effect of the wider green species that suggested a sea posy.

There is an interesting selection of seaweeds here from the fine, delicate, crimson ones to the almost black one in the centre—this, though heavier looking, is not at all thick. A pale background helps to give a watery look and I tried to arrange the posy to look as though it was floating.

as close to it as possible. The piece which includes the rib forms the lower part of the basket, the rib making a firm base. Place the other piece (without rib) directly above–not reversing to match up the veins but so that the veins go off in the opposite direction, thus beginning a woven or zigzag pattern. These two pieces make two thirds of the basket, the top section (without rib) is cut, as just described, from a second leaf and placed in position, ensuring that the veining continues in an alternate direction. If a taller basket is required, it is a simple matter to add more sections.

Cut the sides of the basket to a slight slope; a ruler held across the pieces will keep them in place while you draw a sloping line with a ball point pen, then cut each piece separately. I have tried to cut across all sections at once using a knife, but this is rarely satisfactory. These dry leaves are very brittle and the slightest drag of the knife causes them to break.

## Baskets of Convolvulus Stems

Hollow, twisted convolvulus stems, found in winter when they are just whitened, can make charming baskets with handles. Choose stems from the top of the plant for these are generally the smallest and most weathered.

With a cool iron, press the stems in a curving shape, then cut them into lengths–the size wanted for the length of the basket. Place one piece above another, matching curves. If some curves are not so deep as others it will be found that when it comes to sticking them in place they can be made to close up with a little

pressure of the finger, thus ensuring that the background doesn't show through and spoil the effect.

To make a handle, withdraw some stems from the twisted 'skein' of convolvulus stems leaving only three thin ones still twisted. Iron these into a U shape and cut to size. When the handle is stuck on the picture the ends are not attached to the sides of the basket, but placed slightly higher up, leaving room to fill the basket with flowers without having to stick them on top of the handle.

**To fill the basket** Baskets made of twisted convolvulus have a more substantial look than ones made from leaves, so flowers and foliage of a slightly thicker texture look best, such as heather, bracken, small ivies, anaphalis, kerria, mimosa, solidago and spiraea.

Begin with the line of the arrangement, which in this case is mostly defined by heather foliage. Add other foliage and flowers with stems all directed towards the inside of the basket.

It helps with the effect if a few of the longer stems are cut and placed either side of the handle. Fill the outer edges first. Single flower heads are then used to fill the remaining space and to close the gap between the handle and the basket.

## Pots from Rushes and Grasses

Using their varying shades to advantage, rushes and grasses can be made into pleasing pots or containers for flower arrangement pictures. Collect blades of rush and grass of similar thickness in all the shades that can be found, from almost white, through cream and

*A very realistic basket can be made from the twisted stems of convolvulus.*

*To make a pot from rushes; placing the pattern in position 1. Rushes cut to shape 2.*

74

gold, to almost black. A cool iron or a few days pressing will ensure that they are quite dry.

**To make a pot** Have ready a piece of card roughly the length of the grass blades and a bit higher than the desired height of the finished pot. Place the blades—starting with the darker ones and graduating to the lighter shades—on the card, glueing the tip of each end to hold them in place while you work. If you care to take extra trouble, find blades which in themselves shade from dark to light (this is generally from dark base to lighter tip). Arrange these so that the darker half comes on the left side of the card. When the pot is in place on your picture this will be reversed and the effect will be of light shining on the left with the right side in shadow. If this shading is carried through with the flowers, the result is very rewarding.

Having glued pieces of rush or grass blade to make the desired height of the pot, cut out a simple pot shape from the thinnest manageable paper. Put adhesive all round this pattern about $\frac{1}{2}$ in. from the edge and place it squarely over the grass blades, leave for a day under a weight (blotting paper and a house brick). When quite dry, release the pattern and underlying leaf blades from the piece of card by cutting with a razor blade, leaving just the glued tips still on the card. Then carefully cut round the pattern. The outer $\frac{1}{2}$ in. of the paper pattern is free from adhesive and this is also cut away. The exposed $\frac{1}{2}$ in. of rush or grass blade is then covered with adhesive and the pot is stuck firmly in place on the picture. Leave weighted for a day or so before continuing with the picture.

PAGE 76, TOP
*Not everyone will want to make a landscape picture of plant material but I thought it worth attempting. The background colour took some consideration—eventually a creamy colour was chosen as being fairly neutral, blending well with creams, browns and touches of green.*

*I started the picture by marking out the path and the rounded bank in the foreground with blades of a dark red grass which I found growing in the sand on the Norfolk coast. The horizon came next, marked by two hosta leaves, not used as hills—for which purpose they can be very effective—but the reverse way up, so that the lighter part of the variegation gives a look of water washing over grassy levels. A hill made from an old tulip leaf is placed above on the right. Other tulip leaves make the rolling hills and downs on the opposite side. Below these and the hosta, the gentle slopes are of wild arum spathes, the curved and twisted points adding to the effect. Roughly central are three nettle leaves; two show the paler reverse side, making them seem a little further away. Nettles also make the nearer trees on the left, with little scalloped Nepeta hederacea bushes between them. The effect of darker green undergrowth at the base is obtained with half a horseradish leaf. Thistle leaves make strong lines in the lower left corner and a group of the dark grasses which*

*were used at the beginning of the picture are used upright here. The other side of the path is edged with little clumps of leaves set at an angle, diminishing in size as they recede from the foreground.*

*Strong dramatic leaves on the right bring the picture into focus by their size and colour. The lower reddish ones are from new growth of sycamore and above are the deep blackish-green leaves of elder—these press very dark if new leaves are chosen.*

PAGE 76, BOTTOM
*A still life design in which the texture and a great deal of the intricate beauty of the material is captured. Some white paint is used on the dark background to suggest the top of a stone table or ledge. The bare winter stems of a small vetch provided the curved pieces for the goblet, which is made up of three separate pieces with a small strip for the rim. Skeletonised segments of physalis lanterns curve round it—they are also used to make most of the flowers in the upper right corner, and can be seen placed over hellebore petals on a lower flower. Green florets of hydrangea cluster round the stem of the goblet. Sprigs of alchemilla flowers, trails of reddish sheep's sorrel, and a few damson-coloured honesty pods decorate the table.*

*The flowers above the nest and curving to the left of it were made of acanthus bracts. The creamy white petals with scalloped edges on the table are the outer part of the acanthus flower. Fine grass makes the nest itself with a tiny piece of blackish seaweed to give it depth. The eggs are the little curved shapes found on the seeds of an herbaceous geranium. To the right of the nest and to the left and right among the upper flowers are seed stems of one of the land cresses. Outer seed cases of honesty make the grapes, with a few empty rings from the inner silvery discs for effect. Below are two partly skeletonised holly leaves. Two very chewed up convolvulus leaves, with an insect, made from part of an iris seed case, still busy on them, are just below the nest.*

PAGE 77
*Looking at the work of past craftsmen inspired this design with flowing and curving lines. The use of the down-curving flower on the right and the little intertwining flowers can often be seen in such work. To add to the period look, this design was made on an oval shape which was then mounted on to the blue backing, the colour picking out and emphasising the blue of the delphiniums. The flowers used are between two and three years old, the tulips and delphiniums being among the oldest. The rose petals in the flower at top left are from the variety Alain; they have changed to this very pleasant shade after about two years.*

*Even when many years old, this picture will still be interesting. It is the kind of design seen and appreciated in decorative plaster work and wood inlay, needing little or no colour for effect.*

# Making Flowers from Loose Petals

The pressing papers will hold many single petals owing to the necessity of separating them from their thick centres. Also because many flowers, such as the lily Enchantment, would simply look squashed if pressed complete. Likewise the little tubes of *Lachenalia glaucina* would not press flat if they were left on the stem and so are better pressed separately. Thus there are many different kinds of petals with which to make flower shapes to please ourselves.

In some cases, with flowers such as honeysuckle, daffodil and gaillardia, it may be desirable that they are recognisable in the finished picture, and as long as all the individual parts of the flower were pressed, they can be re-assembled in their own distinctive shape. The first two are best made up in side view; the gaillardia with its blotch of strong colour towards the centre shows up best full faced with an added centre of a much thinner texture than the original, possibly a small bronze-coloured polyanthus.

## Open-faced Flowers

The best way of using some petals, particularly symmetrical ones, is to make them up into a rounded daisy shape. There are some possible variations on this:

**Thin-textured petals**  Petals of a thin texture whose colouring is intensified when placed over a second petal can be used very attractively. If each petal is placed so that it covers about one third of the next, in a circle, the deeper colour where they overlap makes a flower of much more interest than if the petals were just touching. An added centre gives the finishing touch to such a flower. This can be a white Queen Anne's lace floret, or a yellow fennel floret, both have the effect of stamens. Alternatively, a tiny flat flower the same colour as the petals but of a deeper shade gives depth to the centre.

**Thicker-textured petals**  Before simply placing thicker petals in a circle as they are, look at the backs. If the colour is a different shade, lighter or darker, an effect of a double flower is made if the petals are used alternatively, one showing the front, the next the back, and so on. The resulting whirl of shading can be quite striking.

There will probably be petals of different colours from two or three varieties of the same kind of plant. Rudbeckia, for example, will provide plain yellow, yellow blotched crimson, yellow and brown streaked and all brown–all with a texture like very fine velvet. Try putting four of the very dark ones for the lower part of the flower, just slightly to one side, then on each side add two slightly lighter petals and finish off the circle–the upper part of the flower–with the lightest ones. This shading helps to give an illusion of depth to a picture, as though it is being shaded by other flowers above it. For this reason, and because the dark petals give a heavy look, such a flower should be placed low in the arrangement, near the vase or container.

**Petals with dull colouring**  If you have petals which have pressed well, with a nice shape, but which have gone a rather dull, indistinct shade, they can still be used to make an interesting flower. Look for slightly smaller petals of a bright but toning shade, dahlias will often do, and place about five of these over the circle of dull ones. Spaced out so as not to obscure the dull petals, the result can be most pleasing. See bottom picture on page 72.

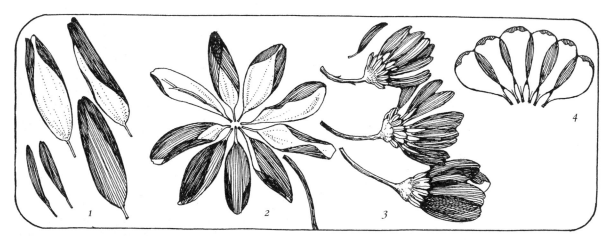

*If flower centres are thick press petals singly 1. These can be used to make a flower 2, or a bud 3. Symmetrical petals look effective slightly overlapped 4.*

## Making Flowers 'Look Up'

To give another dimension to a picture, it is a good idea to include some flowers which have a parasol effect, looking as if the petals curve slightly downwards from a central boss of stamens.

To achieve this, place one straight petal upright, and slightly overlap one on either side of this. Follow up with two or three more evenly on either side, the number will depend on the width of the petals. The last two must not be placed horizontally, but at an angle of 45 degrees curving slightly downwards. A floret of Queen Anne's lace trimmed so that the tiny flowers are left on the upper half only is placed where all the petals meet, the tiny florets protruding above the level of the petals.

## Buds

If buds, half-opened and full-blown flowers of the same variety can be shown (albeit a made-up variety) it gives a flower arrangement a satisfying continuity and avoids a jumbled look. Buds of some of the very small flowers such as helianthemums and rock geraniums can be pressed whole; medium-sized flowers, such as buphthalmum, need to have the buds halved. This can be done with the thumbnails or with a sharp knife. The half bud is then placed on a flat surface, and with a little pressure and a twisting movement of the thumb the tip of the hidden petals is eased to the top of the bud case (the calyx) to show a glimpse of colour.

To provide buds for larger flowers, petals can be used. One is placed with two others—one on either side—almost overlapping it. A calyx of suitable size is put in position at the base of the three petals, as though they were just emerging from it. For narrow buds the calyx can be of primula or polyanthus. To cover the base of wider petals used to make a larger bud, half a calyx from a flower such as hawkweed is suitable.

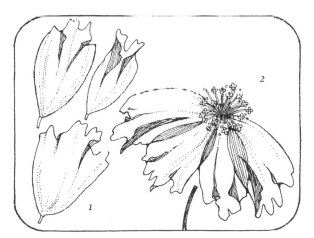

*When pressing petals irregularity of outline is valuable 1. Four petals arranged to make a flower 'look up' 2.*

## Large Single Petals

Large individual petals of tulips, the big colchicums and lilies provide much useful material (see top picture on page 72). The first two have a beautiful silky texture, and the tulips also have some shading. Lilies generally have pleasing shapes and interesting markings, spots and blotches, near the base. A picture can be made using any one of these alone. A simple spray, beautifully made, with one large flower and a smaller half-opened one with a stem and a few well-chosen leaves can make a picture which has a lovely simplicity and shows off the beauty of the petals to advantage.

The shape to make here is something like an exotic paeony, shown in side view. Three of the straightest petals, slightly overlapping, make the far side of the flower. Those with more of a curving shape are then selected and placed evenly on either side, each coming a little lower than the last to form a cup shape, until two petals meet at the base. A centre is placed just above where the petals join, as though you can see into the middle of the flower. Half of an astrantia curved slightly to fit into these lower petals is very effective.

## Versatile Flowers

Some flowers can be made to play a variety of parts. The annual *Salvia horminum* with its coloured petals (strictly speaking, bracts) of deep pink, blue and greenish-white is one of these. It has the added advantage of keeping its colour very well. Tips of the flowers—usually consisting of three petals, two folded with a third between them—and single petals, are pressed. The pink variety is especially useful as fuchsia-shaped flowers can be made from the pressed tips. These are placed in an inverted position and long stamens from fuchsias, rhododendrons or azaleas are hung from them. A more realistic look is given if a longer and slightly thicker stamen is hung below the others to form the stigma. More petals are placed on either side above the tip, generally two are enough, and if the last pair are just overlapped with two narrow petals of a darker red the effect is strengthened.

Pink salvias can also be used to give the appearance of spring blossom. Weathered stems of some of the smaller vetches will press very flat and, as these bear little stalks about $\frac{1}{8}$ in. long where the leaves have fallen, they can be used to support blossom made from pink salvia. This time the tip of the flower is used pointing upwards. If some of these are graduated in size by adding extra side petals and placing them along the upper side of the vetch stem, you have a branch that looks distinctly Oriental, something like cherry blossom.

Charming small butterflies can be made from two single petals of blue salvia. After a time the blue becomes streaked with a lighter colour which fans out from the base of the petal and can look very much like the markings on a wing.

*A stylised vase of flowers with strong lines and colouring, this is over two years old now and has been hung in a subdued light. The vase is part of a lily-of-the-valley leaf, the shaded part having been cut from a second much darker leaf. Both leaves were very thin and were carefully ironed with a cool iron.*

*The spotted orange lily petals, used in threes, have kept their colour well. The two golden flowers of similar shape are made from what were deep bronze tulip petals. The pretty little orchid, Pleione formosanum, on the left, shows some attractive veining. Veining also shows in an open salpiglossis; orange nasturtium petals are to the right of this and a freesia below. Below again, the large exotic flower has dahlia and alstroemeria petals. Dark Salvia fulgens and two beech leaves help with the bold colouring.*

*Most of the flowers are made up of separate petals and this enables the available space to be filled and the curving line to be accentuated where desired.*

*Subtle colouring and simplicity are the striking features of this posy picture. The largest flower is of bleached segments of physalis. These were removed from the bleach before the colour had completely gone; the tips are white but there is still a hint of the orange towards what was the top of the original lantern shape and this helps to give a little shading in the centre of the made-up flower. Single segments are used for a smaller flower and to make the half-open flower on the left. Whisps of silky green grass, bought from the florist, are laid over some of the flowers. Other similar grasses, which have been bleached white, are mixed with the naturally dried hydrangea florets in pale green and delicate purple tones.*

*Bleached sycamore keys make the two lighter iris-type flowers; the darker one on the right has been skeletonised. The little starry daisies dotted about can be found when all the petals are removed from a head of pressed erigeron; they are a shining pale green. Soft, pale purple, wild hare's foot trefoil picks up the shade of some of the hydrangeas. Fine grasses give the upper stems. The lower ones were made by shredding up a dried hollow stem of a large hogweed with a steel comb (the dog's!). These are tied with a gay ribbon of ivory coloured winter grass blades.*

*A flower arrangement on a dark background with highlights of pale gold. The colchicum leaf used for the jug has a sheen which reflects the light, bringing an added interest to the picture. The lower leaves, touched with pink, are from a rose; the smaller darker ones from new growth of Jasminum officinale, which presses to this rich dark brown. The dominant blue flowers will be recognised as florets of delphiniums. Petals of Anemone japonica, some placed with their backs showing, make up*

*the largest pink flowers. Smaller pink flowers higher up are half-opened blossoms of the cherry Hisakura. Top centre are two pinkish flowers from a small wild convolvulus.*

*Three lily petals make up each yellow-spotted tulip-shaped flower and the lovely, silky, pale gold of a marigold is between them. Resting on the rim of the jug the dark velvety crimson flower is made from petals of Pelargonium Black Prince and there is a second flower higher on the right. A greenish hellebore near the handle is surrounded by meadow daisies. The three curving stems which soften the arrangement have little creamy bells of Lonicera pileata hanging from them. Dahlia petals are used for the two fallen flowers; one has a piece of Acer palmatum dissectum atropurpureum leaf at its base.*

*The bee, which I thought was rather successful, has a brown body of a gazania petal striped with pale yellow curls from a chrysanthemum. His wings are pale zinnia petals showing the veining on the backs.*

*As I am fond of painted porcelain, I decided to attempt to create my own decorated vase. Originally, I thought to make the vase shape with curved grasses, but trial and error and some time spent looking through piles of pressed material resulted in a vase made from Dicentra formosa leaves. The leaves were cut in half leaving the thin central rib on the piece to be used, to make the outline more definite. Three pieces in a continuous line make each side, two smaller pieces are used for the base. The dome-shaped lid is three separate pieces. The knob, handles and the shaped base are curls of bracken. These form naturally on the plant during autumn, the leaves curling backwards before disintegrating.*

*The floral decoration helps to round out the body of the vase by the way the flowers are placed—the pansy on the right being slightly elongated as though it was following a curve. To the left is a darker pansy. The spray curving downwards is of amelanchier, picked before the buds opened. The dark miniature roses on the left with a purple hydrangea floret between them, and the two upper pink ones with the side view of a third were chosen because they were a favourite subject of porcelain painters.*

*Surrounding the vase, the pink flowers are from the flowering cherry tree Hisakura—two pressed open, two smaller ones pressed sideways. To make a contrast with the roundness of the cherry, the spiky flowers are made from a base of spider chrysanthemum petals (all pressed singly) with a wild hawkweed placed on top. The result is not bulky as the chrysanthemum petals are tissue thin. Ribes, the flowering currant, with about half the flowers removed, made the pretty sprays in the lower corner, together with rich, dark sycamore leaves. Other leaves on the curving stems are from Clematis montana; choose those which have a bronze tinge on the plant and the colour will deepen in pressing.*

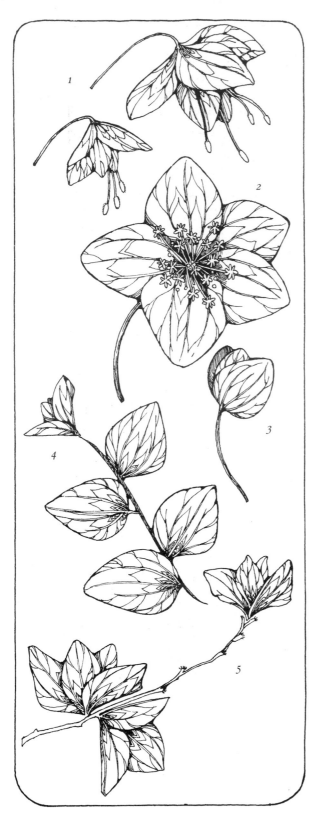

I have also used these blue petals to deepen the colour of a pale blue delphinium. The pressed delphinium is cut in half, and three dark blue petals of salvia are placed so that the lighter petals appear to be emerging from the darker ones at the base.

The greenish-white variety of salvia can do duty as pretty leaves. The shape is suitable, and put on opposite sides of a stem, such as primula or buttercup, they look very attractive on a dark or coloured ground.

## Curved Stems

If a lot of open-faced flowers are included in a picture it tends to have a rather solid appearance. Gently curving stems with small flowers can be made up to fit between the larger ones and curve beyond them, giving a softer, more natural look. Suitable small flowers include tolmiea, lachenalia, yellow and red ribes, verbena, and, for extra tiny ones, single flowers of heuchera or heather.

Any of these can be attached at intervals, either opposite or alternating, to either side of the stem, with a single flower at the top. If sizes can be graduated from smaller ones at the top to larger ones at the base, this adds to the effect.

A pretty result is achieved if the flowers, particularly bell-shaped kinds, are placed on one side of the stem only. This also has the effect of making a stronger curving line.

Another way to get natural touches, and break up an area of large flowers, is to use trails of little flowers. I like the annual verbenas used in this way, particularly the purples, blues and reds. The backs of these are the same shade but much lighter, with a powdery look. 'Growing' on little twisted trailing stems (collected from the new growth of wild convolvulus with a few of its tiny leaves still attached) charming little trails can curve round the foot of a vase or climb up the branches of a tree. If the dark and light shades are used to advantage this can look very realistic.

## General Uses of Loose Petals

Altogether it is very useful to have a collection of many different sizes and shades of single petals, the advantage being that a flower can be made up to fit a given space with more or fewer petals. Spiky shapes can be made to contrast with the more rounded shape of flowers which are usually pressed whole. Shading can be introduced in a picture by making flowers of the same 'variety' but using dark petals for the lower flowers on the right and gradually using lighter ones as they come higher and more to the left.

*Salvia is a versatile flower with many uses: as 'fuchsias' with added stamens 1; as a flower with an added centre 2; as a bud 3; as leaves arranged alternately on a stem 4, and as a spray of spring blossom on a stem of vetch 5.*

# Interesting and Unusual Material

The closer one becomes to Nature (which usually means all growing things) the more one comes to appreciate not only the obvious beauty of petals and leaves, but also the delicate structure of other parts of plants—such as those which bear the seed. There is an amazing variety of shapes and sizes, many with intricate, ingenious ways of discharging their seed. It is usually when all the seed has gone that the winter skeleton of the pod or capsule is thin enough to be pressed. Even then it is generally pressed in separate pieces so that the delicate structure is not obscured. These interesting seedheads can more easily be found on wild plants than in tidy gardens, but it is worthwhile leaving a flower head or two on plants when tidying up the garden, to see if the seedheads have any possibilities. At one time I was very keen on deadheading and removing the last of the dying flowers, not realising that seedheads and winter stems offer such a variety of shapes and textures. Pictures with quite a different kind of beauty can be made compared to those which depend on the subtle colouring and shapes of leaves and petals—delicate pictures with intricate detail which look so charming on coloured grounds, and strong dramatic ones on black grounds.

## Semi-transparent Parts

Some plants have two stages at which they supply interesting material for pressing.

ALYSSUM AND SHEPHERD'S PURSE These plants are similar in that they both have little seed cases borne on either side of the stem; rounded and clustered near the top in the case of alyssum, and angled and reaching further down the stem in the shepherd's purse (*Capsella bursa-pastoris*). With both plants, when the outer cases have fallen away and the seed gone, for a short time (and you have to be quick about this) silvery semi-transparent discs are left. Though the weather soon shatters them, it is possible to find a whole stem intact. They are lovely to use, having a pearly quality, but should you be too late and the silvery membranes have gone, the tiny empty shapes are still beautifully formed, and with a coloured background showing through are most attractive.

HONESTY (Lunaria) This plant is similar to alyssum and shepherd's purse though on a much bigger scale, and here the outer cases as well as the inside can be used. The reddish ones make good plums, damsons or berries, while the green ones give a fair imitation of grapes (see bottom picture on page 76). The silvery inner part can make rounded flower shapes, two layers

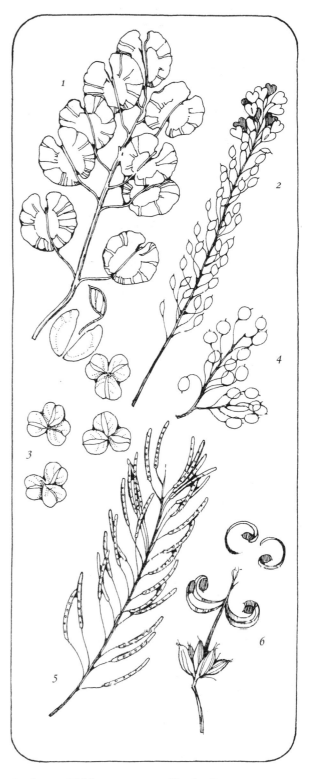

*Seed cases. Field penny cress 1, Shepherd's purse 2, Muscari 3, Alyssum 4, Wild cress 5, Geranium 6.*

of the 'petals' being placed in a circle, the inner ring slightly smaller, arranged so that an inner petal slightly overlaps two of the outer ones at the base. A pressed astrantia flower makes a very suitable centre for these.

The silvery inner parts are also easily shattered, but are not useless even then. Those with ragged bits still attached to the outer rim can be cut lengthwise. Five or six of these placed at the base of a tree to resemble fern leaves are very effective for Oriental pictures on dark backgrounds.

With the silvery discs quite gone, I have used the empty rings—distorting the shape a little—for stepping stones across a dark river.

FIELD PENNY CRESS (*Thlaspi arvense*) In this plant the seedhead has two semi-circular outer cases. Where these are joined to make a circle a little semi-transparent, almost diamond-shaped piece can be found. I have used these as tiny leaves on trees made of fine stems, and they also make very good birds' eyes. The two outer creamy coloured cases may be used as foliage on stylised Oriental trees.

ROSE BAY WILLOW HERB (*Chamaenerion angustifolium*) This plant bears quite a different kind of seed case, long and very slender, and reddish in colour. If the seed cases are gently stroked between the fingers when they are ripe they will spring open to discharge a silky tangle of seeds. I made a picture using them at this stage, but found that it was most convenient to bring them home unopened. I had ready a piece of dark card with a spray of stems already attached. The seed cases were then opened, and although a lot of the seed was lost, enough remained to fan out of the case in a lovely pattern. Tiny spots of adhesive were put on the edges of the cases, which were then quickly put in place on the card. Six or seven seed cases were attached to the stems and the glass was immediately put over the picture and nailed firmly in the frame. A very simple picture but most interesting, and in a way a bit of an experiment, for the fine seeds, not being stuck, may in time come right out of the seed case. But even if this does happen, I am hoping they will look quite effective—as though the wind is blowing them away.

A number of more reliable uses can be found for these outer seed cases when they are really weathered for they twist and curl in perfect curves and circles. Curved ones can be built up to form clouds and used in illustrations for children (see bottom right picture on page 65). If two are placed slightly apart, one a little above the other, they can emphasise the roundness of a bowl. Small bunches of the straighter ones can make the stems for miniature posies. With the circular ones, chains (apparently linked) can be made, perhaps for a hanging basket. Finally, a use I often find for the circular ones is as bubbles in sea pictures, particularly those made from seaweed. See picture on page 73.

THE UMBELLIFERAE FAMILY I must confess that I find difficulty in sorting this family out, many of the plants

*Japanese lacquer and inlaid ivory pictures on a black or very dark red background can be beautiful, with a quality of mystery and stillness—I have tried to create a similar effect in this picture. The river banks and hills are outlined with thin winter stems of Queen Anne's lace, which can be found with lovely curves and strange angles. With these in position I proceeded to 'plant' the banks.*

*The tree first, most important in Oriental pictures and usually a kind of pine. This one is a piece of ivy root, cleaned and bleached and still with the delicate fibrous roots attached which make the intricate little branches. Dandelion clocks and semi-transparent discs from shepherd's purse supply the foliage. Shattered honesty discs cut in half make the fern-like plant at the foot of the tree. In between the petals of dahlia flowers can be found silky pale green petal shapes—these were used for the large flowers on the left, which are finished with a centre of the winter remains of wild carrot flowers. Faded, greenish Chinese lanterns make the leaves, some of which were bleached to a paler shade. Below are curving seedy stems of land cress. Water lilies of hop flowers float on either side of stepping stones made from honesty rings. Little upright bunches of grass blades punctuate the bends of the river, diminishing in size with the distance.*

*Mare's tail looks at home near an Oriental river, lower right. Birds of sycamore keys fly above; the lighter one has been bleached.*

being, to me, so very similar. The familiar ones are Queen Anne's lace (wild parsley), wild carrot and hogweed. Between them they yield a variety of different parts that are suitable for pressing.

Wild carrot flowers can be collected when they first appear, or after the tiny petals fall but before the seeds harden. Both of these stages have a lovely lacy quality. Quite tiny flowers can be found lower down on the plant and it is easy to imagine a peacock's tail made of these.

With Queen Anne's lace the individual florets which make up the flower head are pressed separately, some with their little stalk attached to use as small flowers, others, without the stalks, are indispensable for using as centres for made-up flowers.

When the flowers and seeds have long gone, the winter heads of this family of plants, which will be bleached almost white by November, offer some delicate shapes. Some have five or six little claw shapes where the flowers were, each with its own small stem; these are pressed sideways and make lovely little birds' feet. If they are very dry when picked, a short soaking in warm water will make them pliable and prevent them from shattering. Then place between blotting paper to dry them and press for a week or so.

Other stems have heads with many fine stalks radiating from the centre and may be found bearing the brown skeletons of tiny flowers. Half of one of these makes an attractive shape to use with 'flowers' of similar texture such as golden thistle backs pressed flat.

With the tiny brown flowers removed, the stems from half a head can make a vase, the outer two curving for the sides with three or five left between; any others being cut out. The weathered tall stems of the plant itself assume some very strange shapes. Choose the thinner ones and as they are hollow they will press quite flat. The odd angles that can be found make them useful for indicating the outline of a river. This is shown in the Oriental-type landscape on page 84.

**Other seed cases** Cultivated plants, such as winter aconite, muscari and eucomis, have seed cases which can be used as flower shapes.

ACONITE The seeds are in lovely, pale golden folded cases which are joined for about two-thirds of the length from the base. There are five or six of these in a circle. If any seeds remain, shake them out through the hole in the end of the case and sow them in the garden around the base of trees where they will look perfect in a year or two. Press the separate cases, giving them a start with pressure from the thumb. This will flatten out the folded tube; a little wrap-over piece where the tube-join starts, stays in place. When pressed really flat five cases placed in a circle make a most attractive flower on a dark ground, a pretty pattern showing through where the tiny stalks of each meet in the middle.

MUSCARI AND EUCOMIS These have similar cup-shaped seed vessels composed of three sections joined together. These are opened out and pressed flat, and may be used individually or clustered together as hydrangea-type flowers. The muscari seed case is also small and soft enough to be left unopened and pressed sideways. It makes a small cup or bell when seen from the side view, and looks attractive when placed on the lower side of a curving stem.

**Fluffy seedheads** These, of course, are at their most beautiful when they are a perfect sphere, as in the ordinary dandelion, but some of their lightness and delicacy can be captured in pressing.

DRYAS OCTOPETALA This has fluffy heads which can be cut as soon as they open. Handled carefully, they will not shatter.

HAWKWEED AND COLTSFOOT (Hieracium and Tussilago) The seedheads are impossible to carry home when they are formed, so pick them when the silky heads are only just beginning to emerge. Put the stems in a mixture of 3 parts tepid water to 1 part glycerine. They will flop over the edge of the jar almost immediately but leave them just long enough for the heads to open then remove from the mixture. Cut the stem off (curving scissors make the closest possible cut) and press the heads between blotting paper. Change the paper after two or three days in case any oil comes

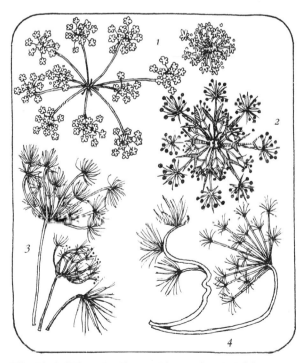

*The Umbelliferae family provides good material for pressing. The flower heads at various stages 1, 2, 3. Weathered winter stems with skeleton seedheads 4.*

*A picture which is pleasing in its simplicity having something of the delicate quality of a dandelion or goat's beard clock. The centre is a pressed* Dryas octopetala *seedhead. When stuck in place, it was gently brushed out with an artist's paintbrush. Round the edges are little single parachutes from a shattered goat's beard seedhead; the seeds have been cut off. Field penny cress supplies the charming little diamond shapes between. Land cress seed stems, with only the inner membrane left, make suitable leaves. The butterfly is four portions of a skeletonised hydrangea floret.*

*Use only sufficient glue to stop the pieces blowing away, or some of the ethereal quality is lost. Then get the glass on this one quickly!*

### Bracts

Both the violet and red forms of *Anemone pulsatilla* (Pasque flower) press to a rather muddy shade, but the lovely bracts behind the flower are worth looking for. A picture in which these are used as a big chrysanthemum-type flower head or purely as a design might, at first glance, be taken for a picture done with chalk, for on a dark background the fine silvery-white hairs on the bracts have a powdery look. A simple design with the minimum of overlapping shows these bracts off to advantage.

### Tendrils

These can give finish to a picture, especially if the design consists only of a few stems of flowers. In such a case the stems are more pleasing when placed at an angle across the background, but sometimes they tend to look as though they are falling. Two curls of tendrils, one small one curled below the larger, placed at the foot of the stems—holding them up as it were—will balance the picture as well as adding interesting detail.

Perfect coils can be found on the wild bryony and also the passion flower. Pick all sizes, from the largest coils of perhaps two rings to the very tight little springs. These last look fine with grapes, and I have also used them for bodies of dragonflies.

When sweet peas have finished their annual flowering they no longer need their little supporting tendrils and these will yield some perfect tiny curls, often in sets of three. You will want to use them, as I do, not because anything in particular can be made from them, but for the absolute precision of their form, which is so satisfying to the eye.

### Grasses

It was not until I came to collect these for use in pictures that I realised how very many different kinds there are. In fact, they comprise one of the largest plant families, varying from those which are much too big and fat to press, to delicate annual grasses. Mostly it is after the seeds have fallen that they will press really

OPPOSITE
*The filigree vase of this design is made from two rotted leaves of horseradish which had such attractive, curving shapes that I pressed them. There is such a wealth of natural material here that it isn't possible to indicate everything. However, among the plant material will be found: an opened flower of chequered* Fritillaria meleagris *with, above, a dried marigold back. Clustered hydrangea florets, Queen Anne's lace and fennel flowers and three tufted sprays of a beige seaweed. Tiny wild convolvulus flowers hang down on the right. Various seed cases and grasses complete the design.*

*All these are laid over a background of skeletonised leaves. The colouring is predominately cream with a range of browns through to black.*

through, but generally there is none. They can be used as soon as they are flat, removing the green backs piece by piece so that the centre remains intact.

GOAT'S BEARD (*Tragopogon pratensis*) This can be used to achieve a lovely misty effect. Use the individual 'parachutes' of the seedheads, that will almost certainly have come to pieces by the time you get them home, placing them round in a circle so that they come just beyond the outer edge of a complete head.

With patience, these separate pieces can also be used to form a sort of dandelion clock, by making circles diminishing in size until the centre is reached, and finishing with a centre of, perhaps, a very small poppy cap.

flat. They then give a lovely airy look, softening the edges of flower arrangement pictures. I press as many of the really fine ones as I can find. In the picture of an arrangement under a dome on page 63 they give an interesting hazy look and help to create the illusion of depth.

### Skeletonised Plant Material

**Leaves** A leaf that has been perfectly skeletonised by the elements is a thing of beauty, to be treasured by child and adult flower arrangers alike. But a perfect leaf is all too rare; most are only partially skeletonised with dried patches obscuring the veining. Fortunately, a lot of this old dried up outer skin can be removed from the leaves. Choose those which are fairly dry and place them in a warm part of the house so that the patches become crisp. Then lay the leaves on a flat surface and with a hard bristle toothbrush tap the patches, first on one side and then on the other. A lot of the patches will be reduced to powder, which can be seen underneath the leaf. Some parts will come quite clear, in other leaves they may be more persistent, in which case a long soak in rain water often helps.

**Physalis** A good substitute for small-sized leaves and one which also makes flower shapes is the orange Chinese lantern, physalis. Collect the lanterns while still orange, and boil them for half an hour in an old saucepan containing one quart of water to which one dessertspoon of washing soda has been added. Allow them to cool in the water and when they can be handled, gently open the end where the segments meet in a point and cut down along a section on the outside of a rib (or join). Do the same to the other sections so that the lantern will open out flat. Remove the berry from the centre and scrape away the fleshy orange part with a blunt knife. It doesn't matter if the sections separate from each other as they can be used singly. When all the colour is removed, rinse in warm water and press between blotting paper.

Single pieces can be attached to a fine stem for use as leaves. Others can make flowers if placed in a circle with a second layer on top. Alternate the petal shapes so that the points come in between and, with an added centre, they make flowers of a gossamer quality.

Some of the lanterns will skeletonise naturally in the garden if left to the weather. These will be more of a golden-brown colour (the boiled ones being lighter). If these natural ones are not perfect they can be used to make opening bud shapes by easing the tips open to remove the berry then pressing the lantern sideways and arranging and folding it so that the outside edges are marked by rib lines.

**Sycamore seeds (keys)** Collect these when they are just turning colour, before they become really dry and brown and drop from the tree. Skeletonise them in the same way as physalis. The hard seed is then cut off and both sides of the wing-shaped piece scraped

and rinsed. Before pressing between blotting paper it is best to reduce some of the thickness from the hard ridge that leads from where the seed was cut off to half way up the 'key', or the pressure will not be sufficiently even for a nice smooth finish.

Sycamore keys can be used to make compound leaves by using five or seven as leaflets. They are also excellent as wings for birds or butterflies.

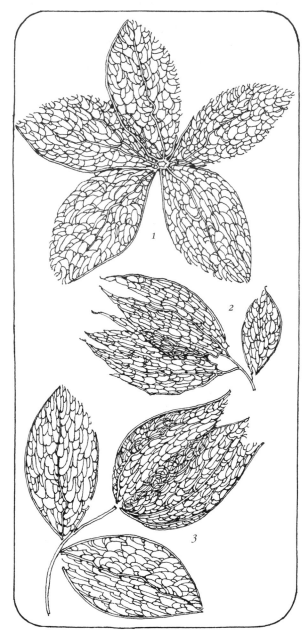

*Physalis. Opened out for a simple flower 1. Unopened capsules pressed sideways 2, 3.*

# Good Plant Material for Pressing

## Cultivated Flowers to Press

ACANTHUS MOLLIS This strange flower, when taken to pieces, gives some interesting shapes and colours to press—some white with brown veining, others of a greenish-purple tinge. Their dry texture makes them easy to use and the colour keeps indefinitely.

ALSTROEMERIA This flower has two kinds of petals, plain rounded ones and veined pointed ones, the latter being the best to use. They can be made up into an exotic-looking flower, the veining lasting well though the main colour fades a little.

ALYSSUM Both the yellow perennial and the purple annual make pretty little sprays when thinned out and keep their colour well.

AMELANCHIER A tallish shrub or small tree with white starry flowers which singly are insignificant but which go slightly creamy and keep a very good shape if pressed in the bud stage.

ANEMONE BLANDA Delicate little blue or pink flowers which can be pressed whole, the overlapping petals making a pleasing pattern.

ANEMONE DE CAEN AND ST BRIGID Colours include reds, blues and purples. Use the front or the silky backs of the flowers. Petals can be pressed separately or the complete flower can be pressed but with the dark stamens removed first.

ANEMONE JAPONICA The semi-double white form presses to a delicate creamy colour and the pink variety keeps very well. These anemones, too, have lovely silky backs.

ANTHEMIS Good yellow petals which keep their colour very well. Press petals separately as the centre is too thick.

AQUILEGIA So far I have only used the long spurs which some varieties have, and find their intriguing shape useful as a contrast to rounded flower shapes.

ASTRANTIA CARNIOLICA Greenish-white flowers with touches of red in the stamens. Press some complete, some with the cushion of stamens removed, and with others, carefully remove each petal shape from the back to leave a fascinating circle of filigree.

AURICULA Many beautiful colours; the yellows keep best, the darker colours press almost black but are useful for shading. The white powder (farina) on the show varieties remains on the petals.

BUPHTHALMUM A very good yellow which keeps well. Press the petals singly.

CHIMONANTHUS FRAGRANS A shrub with strange little spidery flowers of dark purple and pale yellow. Pressed whole they keep most of their colour and, for a long time, their lovely perfume.

CHRYSANTHEMUM The yellows keep the most colour, the darker ones change to shades of bronze and dark brown. Mostly I use the unusual shape of the Spider varieties and the little curls to be found in the centre of the Incurved ones—it does no harm to a cut flower to take a few of these.

CINERARIA A pretty pot plant, of which the richer colours—dark red and purple—are best. (The pinks fade and the white doesn't turn to a good cream.) The petals must be pressed separately because of the thick centres.

CLEMATIS The ones I have used so far are the white Miss Bateman which goes a beautiful old ivory shade, the blue President which takes on an interesting bronze-purple tone and the red Ville de Lyon. All can be pressed whole with the stamens removed.

COLCHICUM The petals of these autumn flowers are best pressed separately. They lose most of their colour but have a lovely silky sheen.

COREOPSIS The petals of this yellow flower have 'movement' in their shape, also pretty indented edges which press in little pleats. The colour keeps extremely well.

*The fascinating detail which can be found when taking an astrantia flower apart.*

DAHLIA Though losing a little of their colour, the veins, unusual shapes to individual petals, and good texture, make these very worth pressing in all shades, the dark red in particular which turns a good purple.

DELPHINIUM One of the best blues of all flowers for keeping. Press whole florets, also single petals which make pretty gowns as they are a useful size, shape and texture for overlapping.

DICENTRA FORMOSA A useful flower which, together with *D. spectabilis*, presses to a rather dullish purple but loses none of its attractive shape.

DICENTRA SPECTABILIS A fascinating locket-shaped flower which, although seeming a little fleshy, does press very well. Tips of stems with four or five flowers graduating in size can be pressed complete and look well in Oriental-type pictures.

ECHINACEA PURPUREA Press the petals singly; they are excellent for texture and for keeping their deep purple-red colour.

ESCHSCHOLZIA This pretty annual poppy presses very well, the white going a good cream, the orange paling a little and the pale purple shade streaking very effectively. Press whole flower open or sideways, also individual petals.

FREESIA May be pressed with one side opened up and spread out to make a vase, or sideways, but remove the stamens first. Most keep a good deal of their original colours though the reds go purple.

FRITILLARIA MELEAGRIS Because of the little bend near the top of the petals these have to be taken to pieces, pressed flat and then reassembled. Three petals will make up the flower's original shape, or extra ones can be added. The chequered appearance stays after pressing, though the paler purple ones go brownish. The very dark ones keep best.

FUCHSIA Taken to pieces these give two different shapes. The colours of some varieties streak a little but this is attractive. They press well having a good firm texture. The stamens are particularly useful for adding to other flowers and for making butterfly antennae.

GENTIANA ACAULIS The large blue trumpets are lovely for vases. Opened out, by cutting up one side, the most interesting markings in the throat can be seen.

HELENIUM Flowers in yellows, bronze and chestnut red. Take the petals, with their pretty scalloped edges, from the thick centres before pressing. The colours keep very well.

HELLEBORE All species are suitable and, in fact, they are some of the best flowers to use for pressing, having a good firm texture and beautiful subtle colouring which lasts very well. Remove stamens from the centre (or just a few, evenly spaced, can be left) and press the complete flower.

HEUCHERA So far I have only pressed the single pink kind. Thin out so that there won't be a muddle of overlapping flowers and press pieces about four inches long. The colour keeps very well and they are pretty for baskets.

HONEYSUCKLE (Lonicera) Press the buds and the open flowers separately. Re-assemble as the original flower or use buds to make a vase and the trumpet-shaped parts to make exotic lily-type flowers.

HYDRANGEA Press florets in all stages of development from freshly opened to dry-textured autumn ones (the last will stand a cool iron if they need a little smoothing). All keep most of their colour which includes white, green and blue, or become a mixture of colours like opals.

HYPERICUM Silky petals when pressed, with an unusual shape suitable for butterflies. The stamens, if carefully removed, can be used in little bunches to make tassels for ribbon ends and pixie hats.

KERRIA JAPONICA Thick little orange-yellow flowers which press quite well if some of the petals are thinned out. A little of the bright colour fades, but they look pretty in baskets.

LACHENALIA GLAUCINA The small bell-shaped flowers are pressed singly sideways. The unusual silvery-blue colour changes very little.

LARKSPUR (Annual delphinium) The pinks and blues are some of the most long-lasting colours for pressing. Press buds as well as whole florets.

LEWISIA The striped varieties of this little rock plant are very pretty. When pressed the silky texture is intensified.

LILY Orange, yellow and bronze varieties are very satisfactory to use, the colours keeping very well. Press separate petals, many of which have pretty veining and spotting.

LOBELIA The trailing blue kind has kept most of its colour for two years so far. The scarlet *Lobelia cardinalis* dulls just a little.

MALOPE The annual mallow with five-petalled, deep rose flowers makes beautiful butterfly wings, the veining adding to the illusion. They darken to a rich purple and have a lovely silky sheen.

MARIGOLD (Calendula) The orange petals fade to a honey colour but are still very pretty, taking on a sheen in pressing. Though thick looking to start with they do press quite flat as the petals become very thin.

MIMOSA (Acacia) Press pieces about three inches long, taking off any of the little ball-like flowers that cross the stem. They look well in baskets made of convolvulus stems.

MONTBRETIA A good orange for keeping. The flowers can be pressed open or sideways.

NERINE UNDULATA This small variety presses well, producing little pink spidery flowers.

PANSY (Viola) The tiny blue and purple ones keep their colour better than the larger varieties; the yellows also last well. Remove the little green backs so that the flowers press flat.

PELARGONIUM The Regal and Zonal pelargoniums provide some of the best red shades for keeping that I have found so far. The rich dark crimson variety Black Prince I have used many times.

PLEIONE FORMOSANUM Press the complete flower sideways. They change to a pretty brown shade with an unusual shape.

PRUNUS HISAKURA One of the popular flowering cherry trees. The flowers are quite lovely pressed whole, fading only a little with the petal edges remaining well defined. Half-open blossoms can be split in half and pressed sideways.

RIBES Both the red and yellow varieties of the flowering currant are very useful if the little bunches are thinned so that excessive overlapping is avoided. Both keep a good deal of their colour.

ROSE As a general rule white roses go a good creamy colour and pinks and reds change to a toffee or deep brown colour. *Rosa mundi* has kept its red and white striping with little loss of colour for over two years so far–the petals make good butterflies.

RUDBECKIA Lovely petals, the yellows and deep brownish bronze keeping their colour for years. Press separate petals from small and large flowers; some of the dark ones have interesting backs.

SALPIGLOSSIS An annual with beautifully veined flowers in many colours. Press the top of the flower cut away from the tube–unless they are to be used as vases–in which case the complete flower should be opened up one side. The main colour pales somewhat but the veining remains.

SALVIA HORMINUM These annuals have white, rose or deep blue bracts which keep their colour well. Press tips of the stem complete with 'flowers', also separate bracts.

SALVIA SPLENDENS It is best to remove the protruding part when pressing the individual flowers. Though most red flowers go brownish, these have kept their colour for over two years.

SALVIA TURKESTANICA The new tips of these plants press to a purple shade, while mature bracts are white shaded pink near the pointed tips. Press them singly.

SOLIDAGO If drastically thinned out, these can be pressed. They keep a good yellow and look well in baskets.

STREPTOCARPUS These flowers, in their various shades of pink, mauve and blue, make pretty vases when opened out and pressed into a fan shape. The markings on the throat help to emphasise the vase shape.

TOLMIEA The little bells have light tips. When pressed separately, they can be arranged along a stem.

TULIP These, I think, improve with age, keeping streaks of their original colour and going wonderfully silky.

VERBENA The tiny flowers of the annual kinds make charming trails when attached to small convolvulus stems. The colours of most appear to keep very well.

WALLFLOWER (Cheiranthus) All the yellows and bronzes keep extremely well. Press complete little florets sideways.

## Cultivated Leaves to Press

Very few leaves are worth pressing for their green colour alone since most of them change to buff and brown shades. Use only those which have interesting shapes to compensate for the loss of colour.

Some brown and bronze leaves lose a little colour eventually, others keep it indefinitely. Grey and silver leaves keep their attractive shades, often becoming silky when pressed. Most yellow leaves are good for three or four years, then pale a little. Red leaves tend to darken.

Unless otherwise mentioned it is best to separate all leaves from their stems before pressing.

ACAENA Small pretty grey leaves sometimes pinkish. Press whole little stems.

ACER PALMATUM DISSECTUM ATROPURPUREUM Very finely divided leaves of purple-brown, suitable for Oriental-type pictures. Small pieces make good bird feathers.

ALCHEMILLA ALPINA This smaller species of lady's mantle has leaves with backs of gleaming silver.

AMELANCHIER A shrub or small tree with striking orange and red autumn colours.

AQUILEGIA Interesting shapes which very often take on a subtle shading of purple-green and yellow.

ARTEMISIA Most species provide good grey or silver foliage. Press tips of three or four inches in length.

ASPHODEL Narrow curvy grey-green leaves useful to give a line to flower pictures.

BEECH (Fagus) Very good at all stages, from thin new leaves to autumn colours.

BERBERIS THUNBERGII Rounded leaves narrowing to a point at the stalk end make the head and beak of a bird. May also be used for hanging 'berries'.

CLEMATIS MONTANA Much of the growth of this climber has a bronze tinge which deepens in pressing. Leaves with a slight twist can suggest the side view of a head.

COLCHICUM If the leaves are left on the bulb they will fade to a golden brown with a lovely silken sheen. They are ideal for making vases.

CYTISUS BATTANDIERI Very beautiful silver-green leaves.

DICENTRA FORMOSA These leaves are lovely when they take on a yellowish tinge in autumn.

EUPHORBIA POLYCHROMA Orange-red autumn colour with leaves so shaped that they can be used as petals.

GERANIUM The varied leaf shapes of the rock garden and herbaceous kinds often have very good autumn colouring.

HAZEL (Corylus) Strong veining gives a pleated look;

the new leaves have an attractive purplish tinge.

HOSTA The variegated ones, though losing their green colour, do keep streaks of shading. When cut in half, they can be used to make hills.

JASMINUM OFFICINALE Press tips with five to seven leaves. The bronzed new growth presses really dark.

NEPETA HEDERACEA VARIEGATA Pretty, mottled, greenish-purple leaves. With their scalloped edges they make effective little bushes.

OPLISMENUS Something like the indoor tradescantia but with narrower striped leaves which make good fish.

PRIVET (Ligustrum) The yellow variety presses to a pleasant gamboge colour.

ROSE The grey-purple and crimson growth on some varieties keeps its colour very well.

SANTOLINA A good silver grey; press tips of about four inches in length.

SENECIO GREYII Grey-green leaves with white felty backs. Either side may be used.

SPIRAEA ANTHONY WATERER Yellow leaves of a good colour and shape can be found towards autumn. Press singly or the tips of shoots with three or four leaves.

VIBURNUM BURKWOODII Autumn finds some very brilliant red leaves with a polished surface; the colour keeps a long time.

VINE (Vitis) There are some beautiful colours to be found in this family. Press tiny leaves for making little trails as well as other sizes.

WILLOW (Salix) Sometimes the leaves have a curved shape which are good for making birds' wings. The silver-grey colour keeps well.

## Wild Flowers and Leaves to Press

This section includes many of the common wild flowers that grow in abundance over the countryside. They are cut down regularly when the hedges and verges are trimmed, so there is no objection to picking a few. But I would like to stress here the importance of picking discriminately and avoiding all the more unusual plants.

ARUM MACULATUM The green spathes of the cuckoo-pint make perfect grassy downs for landscape pictures when cut lengthways and pressed.

BINDWEED (*Convolvulus arvensis*) Little trails, com-

*This was inspired by Oriental flower arrangement and the important feature is the restrained use of flowers which shows the line of the design to best advantage. As there are few flowers they must be of special interest such as these lovely silky tulip petals. They were cream and red when fresh, and most of the red is still there towards the base of the petals. This helps to emphasise the shape of the made-up flower. Two darker petals were used on the largest flower for more depth of colour. The small flowers hanging on twisting stems of convolvulus are Dicentra formosa. Filigree fingers on the bronze Acer palmatum*

*dissectum atropurpureum leaves add a further Oriental touch. They have curving stems of vetch. The five solid dark leaves are of copper beech.*

*The tall vase is rather unusual; it is made from the arum-like spathe of Sauromatum guttatum, which, though reputedly half-hardy, has existed in my rather cold garden for about four years. The cut spathe was rather fleshy and stained the pressing papers with purple-blue dye. I changed the papers often and after about four months it was ready to use. The sides of the vase are the natural edges, but the top and bottom were cut to shape.*

plete with tiny leaves, can be picked from the small pink convolvulus.

BRACKEN Pick all through the season – there are some beautiful shapes to be found. Brown leaves can be lightly ironed.

BRAMBLE The mature leaves have silvery-grey backs. Press also the little tips with three leaflets.

BUTTERCUPS AND CELANDINES While in the pressing papers these stay yellow, but they become quite white after exposure to light. Press spare stems also for use with made-up flowers.

COLTSFOOT (*Tussilago farfara*) Press the centre of these yellow flowers with the thumb first, they will then press flat. The stripy backs are effective.

CRANE'S BILL Pretty little rosy flowers of the wild geranium which are best pressed sideways. They turn to mauve after pressing. The autumn leaf colour is very good.

DAISIES (*Bellis perennis*) Little meadow daisies often with pink edges and backs. Use the backs or fronts, also half-opened flowers divided in two.

ELDER (Sambucus) Look for bronze new growth and press the tips complete with about five leaves.

FENNEL (*Foeniculum vulgare*) Often some of the lower pieces of this feathery foliage go a lovely bronze yellow. Press some of the little individual flowers to make centres for made-up flowers.

GRASSES Choose the most delicate, particularly when the seeds have fallen.

HARE'S FOOT TREFOIL (*Trifolium arvense*) These pinkish-grey, fat little heads press well if picked before they mature and become too hard.

IVY (Hedera) Some beautiful colours are to be found in the wild ivies and a surprising number of different shapes. But I have met some people who consider the plant unlucky and won't buy a picture which has the leaves in it.

MALLOW (Malva) The purple-pink open bell-shaped flowers press well sideways.

MARE'S TAIL (*Hippuris vulgaris*) If collected when young, the smaller ones will press flat. They look well in Oriental pictures and water scenes.

*Bracken provides superb shapes suggesting many uses in pictures and designs.*

MEADOWSWEET (*Filipendula ulmaria*) Small pieces of this foamy flower press to a creamy colour. It is useful in baskets.

MELILOT (Melilotus) Attractive sprays of small yellow flowers which keep very well.

NETTLE (Urtica) Serrated leaves sometimes with a purple tinge make good little trees for landscapes.

OAK (Quercus) Press new small leaves – they are often bronze in colour and slightly curved, and the colour deepens after pressing.

PUSSY WILLOW (Salix) The smaller new catkins cut in half and pressed under a good weight will keep their silky coats.

QUEEN ANNE'S LACE (Wild parsley, *Anthriscus sylvestris*) Single little florets without the small stems are invaluable for centres for made-up flowers. (This applies to all similar plants.)

ROSE BAY WILLOW HERB (*Chamaenerion angustifolium*) Interesting pattern to the flowers which lose a little of their colour when pressed.

SHEEP'S SORREL (*Rumex acetosella*) The stems, with their reddish dots, press well and are most useful.

SILVER WEED (*Potentilla anserina*) Many of these leaves, which have serrated edges, curve beautifully; they keep their silver or pale bronze autumn colour.

SWEET CHESTNUT (*Castanea sativa*) Collect unmarked fallen leaves in the autumn to make attractive baskets.

SYCAMORE (*Acer pseudoplatanus*) The new bronze growth presses very dark with an effective shape.

THISTLE (Cirsium) The leaves, which can be trimmed after pressing, can be used in landscapes. They also fit in well with sea pictures.

VETCH (Vicia) Though the green fades after some time, the dainty curving shapes with little tendrils make them attractive to use.

## Some Flowers to Avoid

For various reasons, such as bad colour, lack of colour or poor shape, the following flowers may be disappointing when pressed: African violets, convallaria, hemerocallis, lapageria, mesembryanthemum, Michaelmas daisies, weigela.

The following go almost transparent after exposure to light: begonia, campanula, lithospermum, mertensia, myosotis, phlox.

The very attractive grasses used in this design were brought home from a holiday in Scotland. When the light catches them, the greenish colour is shot with purple. Their curving tips suggested to me that they could take the place of a petal shape, especially in a flower that normally has a shaggy appearance. So they became chrysanthemums, not obviously, I admit, but they do make a pleasing picture of a different kind.

The bases of pressed erigeron flowers with all the petals removed make the centres. The flowers have been set at an angle as this tends to make a more pleasing design than would a few flowers on stems placed upright. The two curls from bryony tendrils balance and anchor them at the base.

# Index